Verify Before Trust

Navigating the Complexities

Of

Financial Decisions

Andrew J. Pelliccio

Foreword

In life's journey, the transition into retirement is one of our most significant phases. It is a time of reflection, planning, and, most importantly, ensuring that the golden years are as comfortable and secure as possible. As we stand on the threshold of this new chapter, the importance of making informed financial decisions cannot be overstated. Our choices today will shape our tomorrow, determining the quality of life we will enjoy in retirement.

This book is a guide for those preparing for and approaching retirement. It provides a comprehensive overview of investment options tailored to meet the diverse needs of individuals at this crucial stage. A solid understanding of available investment opportunities is essential in a world where financial markets are complex and ever-changing.

Over the years, I have witnessed countless individuals navigating the intricate landscape of retirement planning. Some have done so with confidence, knowledge, and a clear strategy, while others have faced uncertainty and confusion, unsure how to secure their financial future. This disparity underscores the need for a resource that educates and empowers.

These pages provide explanations of various investment vehicles, from traditional options like stocks and bonds to more nuanced choices such as annuities and life insurance. Each chapter is designed to demystify these instruments, breaking down their benefits, risks, and suitability for different financial goals and tolerances.

Beyond the technical aspects, this book emphasizes the importance of a holistic approach to retirement planning. It encourages readers to consider their unique circumstances, aspirations, and risk tolerance when making investment decisions. Whether you are just beginning to think about retirement or are on the brink of this new phase, the insights and strategies presented here will equip you with the tools to make informed choices.

The goal is to transform apprehension into assurance, guiding you toward a future where your financial security is not left to chance but results from deliberate, informed planning. Retirement should be a time of joy and fulfillment, free from the stress of financial uncertainty. By arming yourself with knowledge and understanding, you can take control of your financial destiny and look forward to a future of peace and prosperity.

As you explore the world of investment options, remember that you have the power to shape your retirement.

With best wishes for your financial success,

Andrew J Pelliccio

Verify Before Trust: Navigating the Complexities of Financial Decisions is a comprehensive tool for individuals navigating the intricate world of financial planning and investments. This book aims to equip readers with crucial knowledge and insights before engaging with a financial advisor and delving into various available investment products.

The book explores annuities, breaking down their types—from fixed and variable to indexed—and meticulously explains their potential roles in a well-rounded investment portfolio. It illuminates the advantages and disadvantages, helping readers discern which annuity aligns with their financial objectives.

Verify Before Trust examines various life insurance products and emphasizes the importance of understanding them as safety nets and potential components of a strategic investment plan.

As the journey through investment options continues, the book delves into a spectrum of long-term and short-term investment vehicles. It covers traditional investments like stocks, bonds, gold, alternative investments, and more contemporary options like real estate investments. The guide offers pragmatic information on evaluating these opportunities, considering personal financial goals, risk appetite, and market conditions.

A key focus of *Verify Before Trust* is the critical process of choosing and collaborating with a financial advisor. The book empowers readers with the right questions to ask, highlights warning signs to watch out for, and underscores the significance of understanding fee structures, advisor qualifications, and fiduciary responsibilities.

Verify Before Trust is meant to help the reader understand the need for due diligence before choosing an advisor and investment options.

Verify Before Trust offers practical tips and accessible explanations, making it a vital resource for anyone aspiring to make informed, confident decisions about their financial future. It's an essential read for investment novices and those seeking to enhance their understanding of the complex financial landscape.

Verify Before Trust is NOT financial advice. It is a broad view of some investment options available to aid in basic knowledge of options.

People spend their lives mastering their trade or building a business, becoming experts at their vocation. This informational book is a quick reference, as most selections are personal and decided after meeting with a financial advisor. Meeting with an advisor should not be the first time options are considered.

Verify Before Trust aims to help the reader become a more informed customer when meeting with an advisor.

Verify Before Trust was partially developed using AI research tools and publicly available information to provide an educational perspective on the role of various investment options in retirement income planning. The content reflects general knowledge and widely accepted principles related to investment types, their benefits, risks, and considerations. It is important to note that AI tools do not inherently provide specific source information or citations for the material presented.

The information in this book is for educational and informational purposes only and should not be considered financial, investment, or insurance advice. It does not replace the need for personalized advice from a qualified professional. While every effort has been made to present accurate and up-to-date information, financial products and strategies vary significantly based on individual circumstances, goals, and regulatory environments. Readers are strongly encouraged to consult a licensed financial advisor and/or insurance professional to discuss their unique financial needs and determine the most appropriate options.

"Beware of the cuff links."

Thank you, Cousin Michael, for the quote

Monogrammed shirts and fancy cars may indicate an advisor's success. However, be informed, understand the options, and always ensure they prioritize your best interests, not the best commission. When an advisor provides documentation, read every page. Never allow pressure. Take note of the fine print and ask questions.

Contents

CHECK LIST

Checklist of Key Items to Review when Purchasing an Alternate Investment

Checklist of Key Items to Review When Seeking Professional Investment Advice

Checklist of Key Items to Review When Considering Investment Options

Checklist of Key Items to Review when Considering a CD Investment

Checklist of Key Items to Review When Considering a Real Estate Investment

Checklist of Key Items to Review When Considering Taking Social Security

Checklist of Key Items to Review when Considering a 401K or an IRA

Checklist of Key Items to Review When Considering Taking Medicare

Checklist of Key Items to Review When Considering Estate Planning

Checklist of Key Items to Review When Considering Saving for Children Education

Checklist of Key Items to Review When Considering College Savings Plans

Checklist of Key Items to Review When Considering Gold Investment

Checklist of Key Items to Review When Considering Growth Options for Retirement Savings

Checklist of Key Items to Review When Considering Using the Wall Street Approach

Chapter 1
Understanding Annuities

Navigating retirement income planning can be intimidating, yet the key lies in effectively utilizing available resources. Regarding retirement planning, annuities can be a valuable tool in certain situations. However, due to the significant financial implications, seeking advice from a financial advisor before making any major commitments is crucial.

Determining whether an income gap during retirement needs to be filled is a fundamental step. Annuities are designed to augment income from reliable sources like pensions or Social Security. Exploring alternatives such as annuities or other investments becomes essential if retirement expenses exceed these sources.

It's diligent to scrutinize financial advisors' advice, especially regarding annuities. While they may not always be the optimal growth option, they can offer a reliable income stream. The allure of annuities often lies in their promise of "guaranteed income." However, to avoid financial inefficiencies, it is necessary to ensure that the amount aligns with actual needs.

Fixed annuities guarantee a steady income, while variable annuities' payments can vary depending on market conditions. Before you decide to invest in annuities, comprehensive planning is essential. This involves assessing your current and future financial situation, estimating your retirement income, and considering unexpected expenses. Evaluating your interest in alternative income strategies, such as investments, is also important. A skilled financial planner can help you develop a strategy that meets your income needs and can adapt to potential surprises.

When considering annuities, it's important to ensure that the advice you receive from your financial advisor is truly in your best interest. Be aware of any potential conflicts of interest or undisclosed incentives that may influence their recommendations.

Pay attention to the details of annuity products, including surrender charges, and understand the options for accessing funds if needed. Spreading annuity purchases across multiple companies can enhance security. Be mindful of state protection caps and the financial strength of the insurance providers. Always ask the advisor.

Ensuring access to liquid assets outside of annuities and investments is prudent. A well-rounded, growth-focused, conservative retirement plan should offer financial access when required. Annuities may be a component in investors' toolkits, particularly those planning for retirement. Understanding annuities is important for any investor looking to manage financial risk by using them and ensuring a stable income stream in their post-working years. At its core, an annuity is a financial product typically provided by an insurance company and designed to offer a steady income stream for a set period or the individual's lifetime.

For investors, annuities serve several purposes. First, they act as a hedge against outliving one's savings, providing a guaranteed income irrespective of market fluctuations or the individual's lifespan. This is particularly valuable in an era of increased life expectancy and uncertain economic conditions. Second, annuities can be structured in various ways, allowing investors to tailor them to specific needs— whether seeking immediate income or planning for future financial stability.

However, the complexity of annuities — including their fee structures, tax implications, various riders, and options — makes it imperative for investors to thoroughly understand them before committing. The choice between immediate and deferred annuities, fixed versus variable returns, and the implications for estate planning are just a few considerations that must be weighed. In sum, while annuities can be a powerful tool for financial planning, they require careful consideration and, often, guidance from a professional advisor.

1.1. Introduction to Annuities

An annuity is a financial contract between an individual and an insurance company designed to provide a regular income stream over a specified period, often throughout retirement. It is a crucial financial instrument for those looking to secure their financial future. Annuities offer a way to ensure a steady cash flow, which can be particularly valuable during retirement, when one's regular income from employment may cease.

There are several key components to understand about annuities:

- **Principal**: The initial amount of money you invest in the annuity.
- **Payments**: The periodic disbursements made by the insurance company to you, typically monthly, quarterly, or annually.
- **Earnings**: The interest or investment gains earned on your principal amount.
- **Payout Period**: The duration over which the annuity payments will be made, which can be for a fixed period or the rest of your life.

1.2. Pros and Cons of Annuities

Pros:

- **Guaranteed Income:** Annuities offer a reliable source of income, ensuring you won't outlive your savings.
- **Tax Deferral:** Earnings in an annuity grow tax-deferred until withdrawal.
- **Diverse Options:** Different types of annuities allow you to choose what suits your financial goals.

Cons:

- **Fees:** Annuities can have various fees, including surrender charges, administrative fees, and underlying investment fees.

- **Lack of Liquidity:** Many annuities limit access to your principal or may charge penalties for early withdrawals.
- **Inflation Risk**: Fixed annuities may not keep pace with inflation, potentially eroding your purchasing power.

1.3. Types of Annuities in the United States

- **Fixed Annuities** offer a guaranteed interest rate and provide a stable income stream. However, they may not keep up with inflation.
- **Variable Annuities**: These allow you to invest your money in various sub-accounts, like mutual funds. The income you receive depends on the performance of your chosen investments, making it riskier but potentially more rewarding.
- **Indexed Annuities** link your returns to a specific index, like the S&P 500. While they offer growth potential, they often come with caps or limits on your gains.

1.4. Laws Governing the Sale of Annuities

The sale of annuities is regulated at both federal and state levels. These regulations protect consumers from deceptive practices and ensure that annuities are suitable for the individuals purchasing them. Laws and regulations require financial professionals to meet certain standards and disclose all pertinent information about the annuity being sold.

1.5. Annuity Investment vs. Stocks

Comparing annuities to stock investments involves evaluating risk, return, and financial goals. Annuities provide safety and guaranteed income, making them suitable for risk-averse investors. On the other hand, stocks offer higher growth potential but come with greater volatility and uncertainty.

The choice between annuities and stocks depends on your individual financial circumstances, including:

- **Risk Tolerance**: Assess how comfortable you are with market fluctuations.
- **Time Horizon**: Consider your investment horizon, especially if you plan for retirement.
- **Financial Goals**: Determine whether your primary objective is income, growth, or a balance of both.

1.6. Borrowing Ability of Annuity

Some annuities allow you to take loans against the cash value within the contract. This can provide liquidity in times of need. However, borrowing against an annuity comes with costs, such as interest, and can impact your future annuity payments.

1.7. Tax Consequences of Withdrawal of Annuity vs. Loan on Annuity

Withdrawing money from an annuity may trigger taxes, including income tax and potential penalties if you are under the age of 59½. Conversely, loans from annuities are generally not taxable, but they accrue interest that needs to be repaid.

1.8. Annuities for Seniors

Annuities can be particularly attractive for seniors looking to secure their retirement income. The assurance of regular payments can offer peace of mind and financial stability during retirement years. However, seniors must consider their individual circumstances and financial goals before investing in an annuity. Here are some general recommendations for seniors considering an annuity:

- **Immediate annuities**: An immediate annuity can provide a guaranteed income stream for seniors nearing retirement or already retired. Immediate annuities can be particularly useful for seniors who need this income to supplement Social Security or a pension.

- **Fixed annuities**: Fixed annuities offer a guaranteed rate of return and can provide seniors with a stable source of income. They are generally considered low-risk investment options and can provide a sense of security for risk-averse seniors.
- **Longevity annuities**: Longevity annuities are immediate anniversaries that begin paying out at a future date, typically after age 80. They can be a good option for seniors concerned about outliving their savings.

Consider the insurance company's creditworthiness: When purchasing an annuity, it is important to consider its creditworthiness. The company will be responsible for making the income payments to seniors. Therefore, it is best to research the company and its financial stability before investing.

Be aware of the terms and conditions: Before investing in an annuity, it is important to know the terms and conditions, including any fees, penalties, and the insurance company's creditworthiness. It is advisable to consult with a financial advisor or professional to understand the annuity's terms and conditions and determine if it suits your individual circumstances and financial goals.

It is important to note that annuities are long-term investment products and may not be suitable for all investors. They are not typically liquid investments and can be subject to surrender charges if you withdraw the money before the annuity matures. Annuities are also subject to different tax rules than other types of investments.

1.9. Types of Fees in Annuities

Annuities are complex financial products that come with various fees. The fees that may be included in an annuity can vary depending on the type of annuity and the insurance company that issues it. Here are some common types of fees that may be included in an annuity:

- **Sales charges or commissions**: These fees are paid to the insurance agent or financial advisor who sells the annuity.

They can be a one-time fee or a percentage of the premium paid.

- **Mortality and expense risk charges**: These charges cover the insurance company's costs of providing the annuity. They are typically a percentage of the premium paid and are deducted from the annuity's account value.
- **Surrender charges**: Surrender charges are imposed when the contract holder withdraws money from the annuity before a certain period, usually between 5-10 years. The charges can be a percentage of the withdrawal amount and decrease over time.
- **Administrative fees**: These cover the insurance company's expenses for administering the annuity, such as mailing statements or maintaining records.
- **Premium taxes**: Some states impose taxes on the premium paid for an annuity.
- **Rider fees**: Some annuities may include riders, which are optional features that provide additional benefits to the contract. Riders, such as long-term care or death benefit riders, may incur additional fees.

It is important to be aware of all the fees associated with an annuity before investing, as they can significantly impact the return on the investment. It is advisable to consult with a financial advisor or professional to understand the fees associated with an annuity and determine if it suits your financial goals.

1.10. Types of Riders Available for Annuities

Annuity riders are optional features that can be added to an annuity contract to enhance the benefits provided by the annuity. The types of riders available for annuities can vary depending on the insurance company and the type of annuity. Here are some common types of riders available for annuities:

- **Guaranteed income rider**: Provides a minimum income regardless of market performance.
- **Guaranteed minimum withdrawal benefit rider**: This rider guarantees a minimum withdrawal amount for a certain period, regardless of the performance of the underlying investments.
- **Guaranteed minimum income benefit rider**: This rider guarantees a minimum income for a certain period, regardless of the performance of the underlying investments.
- **Guaranteed minimum accumulation benefit rider**: This rider guarantees a minimum accumulation amount, regardless of the performance of the underlying investments.
- **Long-term care rider**: This rider benefits the contract holder if they need long-term care, such as in-home or nursing home care.
- **Death benefit rider**: This rider benefits the contract holder's beneficiaries in the event of the contract holder's death.
- **Chronic illness rider**: This rider provides benefits if the contract holder becomes chronically ill and can no longer perform activities of daily living.
- **Return of premium rider**: This rider returns all or a portion of the premium paid for the annuity if the contract holder dies before a certain age or period.

It is always best to consult with a financial advisor or professional to understand the fees, including rider fees, associated with an annuity and determine if they suit your financial goals.

1.11. Annuity to Supplement a 403(b) Plan

A 403(b) plan is a tax-advantaged retirement savings plan available to employees of public schools and certain tax-exempt organizations. An annuity can provide a guaranteed stream of income, which can help supplement the income from a 403(b) plan. When considering an annuity to supplement a 403(b) plan, it is important to consider the individual's retirement goals, risk tolerance, and overall financial situation.

It's always best to consult with a financial advisor or professional to determine if an annuity is a suitable option to supplement a 403(b) plan and to understand the tax implications. Unlike contributions to a 403(b) plan, annuity contributions are not tax-deductible. It is also important to note that the IRS limits contributions to a 403(b) plan.

1.12. Converting a 403(b) Plan to an Annuity

It is possible to convert a 403(b) plan to an annuity, but it is important to consider the potential benefits and drawbacks of such a conversion. A 403(b) plan is a tax-advantaged retirement savings plan available to employees of public schools and specific tax-exempt organizations. On the other hand, an annuity is a contract between an individual and an insurance company in which the individual makes a lump sum payment or a series of payments to the insurance company in exchange for regular income payments.

Converting a 403(b) plan to an annuity can provide a guaranteed income stream in retirement, which can be useful for supplementing the income from a 403(b) plan. However, it is important to consider the individual's retirement goals, risk tolerance, and overall financial situation when deciding if an annuity is a suitable option.

It is also important to consider the fees and expenses associated with the annuity and the insurance company's creditworthiness, as they can significantly impact the return on the investment. Additionally, understanding the tax implications of the conversion is crucial, as annuities are subject to different tax rules than other types of investments.

It's always best to consult with a financial advisor or professional to understand the tax implications and potential benefits of converting a 403(b) plan to an annuity. They can help evaluate the advantages and disadvantages of such a conversion and assist in making an informed decision that aligns with your retirement goals and financial situation.

A 403(b) plan is a tax-advantaged retirement savings plan available to public school employees and certain tax-exempt organizations, such as non-profit hospitals, churches, and charitable organizations. It is similar to a 401(k) plan, which is available to employees of private companies.

With a 403(b) plan, employees can contribute a portion of their salary on a pre-tax or after-tax (Roth) basis, and the money in the plan grows tax deferred. Employers may also make contributions to the plan on behalf of the employees. The contributions and earnings are not taxed until they are withdrawn, which usually occurs during retirement. Withdrawals before age 59½ may be subject to a 10% penalty tax, with some exceptions.

The IRS sets the contribution limits for 403(b) plans, which are subject to change over time. For example, in 2022, employees could contribute up to $19,500 under age 50 and up to $26,000 if they were 50 or older.

Employees have various investment options, including mutual funds, annuities, and bonds. The investment options and fees vary depending on the plan and the provider.

It's always best to consult with a financial advisor or professional to understand the plan's terms and conditions and determine whether it's a suitable option for your circumstances and financial goals.

1.13. Consequences of Converting a 403b to an Annuity

One of the main benefits of converting a 403(b) plan to an annuity is that it can provide a guaranteed income stream in retirement, which can be useful for supplementing the income from a 403(b) plan. An annuity can also provide a sense of security for risk-averse individuals.

However, several drawbacks must be considered when converting a 403(b) plan to an annuity:

- **Reduced flexibility**: Once individuals convert their 403(b) plan to an annuity, they lose the flexibility to make additional contributions or change investment options.
- **Surrender charges**: Annuities often have surrender charges if an individual withdraws money from the annuity before a certain period of time, usually between 5-10 years.
- **Reduced liquidity**: Annuities are not typically liquid investments, which means it can be challenging to access the funds in an annuity without incurring penalties or charges.
- **Reduced investment growth potential**: Annuities typically have lower returns than other types of investments, such as stocks and bonds, resulting in reduced investment growth potential over the long term.
- **Tax implications**: Annuities are subject to different tax rules than other types of investments, which can result in different tax implications.

It's important to weigh the potential benefits and drawbacks of converting a 403(b) plan to an annuity and consider the individual's retirement goals, risk tolerance, and overall financial situation before deciding. It's always best to consult with a financial advisor or professional to understand the tax implications and potential benefits and drawbacks of converting a 403(b) plan to an annuity.

1.14. Annuity vs. Stock Market Considerations for Retirees

Retirees have different financial goals and risk tolerances than those who are still working and saving for retirement. Investing in an annuity or the stock market will depend on an individual's retirement goals, risk tolerance, and overall financial situation.

Annuities can provide a guaranteed income stream in retirement, supplementing income from other sources such as Social Security and pensions. They can also provide a sense of security for risk-averse individuals. However, annuities often have high fees and expenses, which can limit access to funds in the future.

On the other hand, the stock market can provide the potential for higher returns over the long term, but it also comes with higher risk. Investing in the stock market can effectively grow retirement savings and keep up with inflation. However, it is important to diversify investments and have a long-term investment horizon.

Retirees should consider their retirement goals and risk tolerance when deciding whether to invest in an annuity or the stock market. It's always best to consult with a financial advisor or professional to understand each option's potential benefits and drawbacks and determine whether they suit their circumstances and financial goals.

It's also important to remember that a diversified portfolio that includes a mix of annuities, stocks, and other types of investments may provide the best outcome for retirees.

1.15. Percentage Allocation to Secure Annuity Investment vs. Stock for Retirees

The best percentage allocation to secure annuity investment versus stock for a retiree will depend on the individual's retirement goals, risk tolerance, and overall financial situation.

A secure annuity investment can provide a guaranteed stream of income in retirement, supplementing income from other sources such as Social Security and pensions. Annuities can also provide a sense of security for risk-averse individuals. Therefore, a significant percentage of a retiree's portfolio should be allocated to secure annuities, such as fixed or immediate annuities.

However, retirees should also have some exposure to the stock market, as it can provide the potential for higher returns over the long term and help them keep up with inflation. A well-diversified portfolio that includes stocks, bonds, and other types of investments is generally recommended for retirees.

A general rule of thumb is to allocate a percentage of investments to an annuity equivalent to one's age. For example, a retiree who is 70 years old should allocate 70% of their portfolio to a fixed or immediate annuity and 30% to other types of investments.

As retirees age, they should consider shifting their portfolios towards more secure investments, such as fixed annuities, to ensure a steady income stream during their retirement years.

It is always best to consult with a financial advisor or professional to understand each option's potential benefits and drawbacks and determine whether they suit your circumstances and financial goals.

1.16. Investment in Annuity or Stock During a Down Market

Investing in annuities or stocks during a down market can be challenging, as the value of investments may decrease, and it can be difficult to predict when the market will recover. However, there are a few things to consider when deciding.

For annuities:

- Annuities can provide a guaranteed stream of income, which can be useful for risk-averse investors looking for a more secure investment option during a down market.
- Consider investing in fixed annuities, which provide a guaranteed rate of return, rather than variable annuities, which are tied to the performance of underlying assets.
- Remember that annuities can have high fees and expenses, significantly impacting the return on investment.

For stocks:

- Stocks can be a good investment option during a down market as they are often undervalued, and they may provide higher returns in the long term as the market recovers.

- Consider dollar-cost averaging, a strategy of investing a fixed amount of money at regular intervals, regardless of market conditions. This can help reduce the risk of investing a large sum of money at the wrong time.
- Remember that stocks can be volatile and may not recover as quickly as expected, so it's important to have a long-term investment horizon and diversify your investments.

During a down market, it is essential to be cautious and avoid making impulsive investment decisions. Instead, take the time to evaluate your current financial situation, goals, and risk tolerance.

It is always best to consult with a financial advisor or professional to understand each option's potential benefits and drawbacks and determine whether they suit your circumstances and financial goals.

1.17. Choosing a Financial Advisor or Annuity Broker

Choosing a financial advisor or annuity broker can be challenging, as many options are available. It is important to find one who is trustworthy, experienced, and knowledgeable. Here are some steps to help you choose the best financial advisor or annuity broker:

- **Research potential advisors**: Check online resources, such as the Financial Industry Regulatory Authority (FINRA) website, to determine if the advisor is registered and in good standing with the appropriate regulatory bodies.
- **Ask for referrals**: Ask friends, family, or other professionals for recommendations on advisors they trust.
- **Check qualifications**: Look for advisors with relevant professional designations, such as the Certified Financial Planner (CFP) or Chartered Financial Analyst (CFA) designations, indicating that the advisor has met specific educational and experience requirements.

- **Look for transparency**: Work with advisors who are transparent about their fees and services and who explain their investment strategies clearly and understandably.
- **Assess compatibility**: Meet with potential advisors to assess their communication style, investment philosophy, and overall approach to client collaboration. Ensure you feel comfortable with the advisor and believe they will have your best interests in mind.
- **Ensure they are licensed**: Verify that the advisor is authorized to sell annuities in your state.

Working with an advisor who can help you understand the complex and ever-changing annuities market is also essential. They should be able to explain the diverse types of annuities, their benefits and drawbacks, and how they align with your personal goals and risk tolerance.

It is always best to consult with a financial advisor or professional to understand each option's potential benefits and drawbacks and determine if they suit your circumstances and financial goals.

Chapter 2
Life Insurance Options

Understanding life insurance options is an integral part of comprehensive financial planning for investors. Life insurance is a contract between an individual and an insurance company designed to provide financial protection to the policyholder's beneficiaries in the event of the policyholder's death. This understanding is crucial not just for personal financial security but also for ensuring the well-being of dependents.

Life insurance can serve multiple purposes in an investment portfolio. Firstly, it offers peace of mind, knowing that loved ones will have financial support in case of the policyholder's untimely demise. This is particularly important for individuals with dependents who rely on their income. Secondly, certain life insurance policies, such as whole life or universal life, can also function as investment tools, accumulating cash value over time that the policyholder can borrow against or use for other financial needs.

However, the world of life insurance is complex, with various options available, each with its own set of features, benefits, and costs. Term life insurance, for instance, offers coverage for a specific period and is generally more affordable, while whole life insurance offers lifelong coverage with an investment component. Universal life insurance adds the flexibility of adjustable premiums and death benefits. Understanding these options, their tax implications, and how they align with one's overall financial goals and risk tolerance is vital for making informed decisions.

While life insurance is critical for risk management and financial planning, investors must carefully evaluate their options to choose the right type and amount of coverage. This often involves seeking advice from financial advisors to ensure the strategy aligns with broader investment goals and family needs.

2.1. Introduction to Life Insurance

Life insurance is a financial product designed to provide a death benefit to beneficiaries upon the policyholder's death. It serves as a vital tool for protecting loved ones and ensuring their financial security in the event of the policyholder's passing. Life insurance comes in various forms, each tailored to specific needs and circumstances.

2.2. Types of Life Insurance

There are several types of life insurance policies available, each with its own features and suitability:

- **Term Life Insurance**: Term life insurance provides coverage for a specified term, typically 10, 20, or 30 years. It offers a straightforward death benefit without any cash value component. Term policies are generally more affordable and are ideal for those seeking temporary coverage for financial responsibilities like mortgages or education.
- **Whole Life Insurance**: Whole life insurance is a form of permanent life insurance that offers lifelong coverage. It accumulates a cash value component over time, which grows tax-deferred and can be borrowed against or withdrawn, often with tax advantages. Whole life insurance premiums are typically higher than term insurance but remain level throughout the policyholder's life.
- **Universal Life Insurance**: Universal life insurance is another type of permanent insurance that provides flexibility in premium payments and death benefits. Policyholders can adjust premiums and death benefit amounts based on their evolving needs. Universal life insurance also includes a cash value component that can be invested in various accounts, subject to certain interest rates.
- **Variable Life Insurance**: Variable life insurance combines the death benefit with investment opportunities. Policyholders

can invest in sub-accounts similar to mutual funds, which can potentially result in higher cash values and death benefits. However, it also exposes the policyholder to market risk.

- **Variable Universal Life Insurance**: This policy combines universal life insurance features with investment options similar to variable life insurance. Policyholders can adjust premium payments, death benefits, and investment allocations. Investment performance impacts the policy's cash value and death benefit.

2.3. Explanation of Types of Life Insurance

- **Term Life Insurance**: Term life insurance is the simplest form, providing pure life insurance coverage without a savings component. It is suitable for those who need coverage for a specific period, such as while raising children or paying off a mortgage. Term policies offer high coverage amounts at a lower premium cost.
- **Whole Life Insurance**: Whole life insurance offers lifelong coverage with level premiums. A portion of the premium payments goes into a cash value account that grows over time. Policyholders can access this cash value through loans or withdrawals, which can be tax-advantaged.
- **Universal Life Insurance**: Universal life insurance offers flexible premiums and death benefits, making it suitable for individuals with changing financial circumstances. The cash value component earns interest at a rate set by the insurer and can be adjusted within certain limits.
- **Variable Life Insurance**: Variable life insurance allows policyholders to invest in sub-accounts, including stocks, bonds, and other investments. The cash value and death benefit can vary based on the performance of these investments, making it more suitable for those comfortable with investment risk.

- **Variable Universal Life Insurance**: This type of policy combines the flexibility of universal life with the investment opportunities of variable life insurance. Policyholders can adjust premiums, death benefits, and investment allocations as needed. However, it carries both market risk and the risk of lapsing if the cash value is insufficient to cover premiums.

2.4. Usual and Customary Eligibility to Acquire Life Insurance

To acquire life insurance, individuals typically need to meet certain eligibility criteria, which may include:

- **Age**: Most policies are available to individuals within a certain age range, typically 18 to 80 years, although the exact age limits can vary by insurer and policy type.
- **Health**: Insurers often require applicants to undergo a medical examination or answer health-related questions. Health status can influence the premium you pay.
- **Lifestyle**: Some insurers consider lifestyle factors such as smoking, occupation, and participation in high-risk activities when determining eligibility and premium rates.

2.5. Can I Sell My Life Insurance Policy Even if It Is a Term Policy?

While it is possible to sell a life insurance policy, the process, known as a life settlement, is more common with permanent policies like whole life or universal life. Term life insurance policies typically do not have a cash value component, making them less suitable for life settlements.

2.6. What Is a Life Settlement or Viatical Settlement? Why Is This So Important?

A life settlement is a financial transaction in which the policyholder sells their life insurance policy to a third party for a lump sum cash payment. The buyer takes over the premium payments and becomes the policy's beneficiary, receiving the death benefit upon the policyholder's passing.

Viatical settlements are a type of life settlement in which individuals with terminal or chronic illnesses sell their life insurance policies to access funds for medical expenses and other needs. These settlements allow policyholders to unlock the value of their life insurance policy while they are still alive, providing financial relief when it's needed most.

2.7. Most Common Mistake

One of the most common mistakes individuals make regarding life insurance is underestimating their coverage needs. Failing to adequately assess financial responsibilities, such as mortgage payments, education costs, and ongoing living expenses, can lead to inadequate coverage. Conversely, overestimating coverage needs may result in unnecessarily high premiums.

It's important to note that life settlements are unsuitable for everyone and should be carefully considered. Factors such as the policyholder's age, health, and policy terms can all impact the policy's value in a life settlement. Consulting with a financial advisor or attorney before selling a life insurance policy through a life settlement is recommended.

2.8. Viatical Settlement Brokers

Viatical settlement brokers specialize in facilitating the sale of life insurance policies in a life settlement or viatical settlement transaction. They work with both policyholders selling their life insurance policies and investors looking to purchase policies for their investment portfolios.

The role of the viatical settlement broker is to assess the policyholder's life insurance policy and determine its potential value in a life settlement, help the policyholder find a suitable buyer, and negotiate the terms of the sale.

Viatical settlement brokers typically receive a commission, which is a percentage of the life insurance policy's sale price. It is important to choose a reputable and experienced viatical settlement broker to ensure a fair and transparent transaction. Policyholders should also thoroughly review and understand the terms of any agreement before proceeding with a life settlement.

You can find viatical settlement brokers by searching the internet, asking for referrals from financial professionals or industry organizations, or checking with the National Association of Viatical Settlement Companies (NAVSC). It is important to thoroughly research and compare multiple options to find a reputable, experienced broker who meets your needs and requirements.

2.9. Bundled Life Insurance for Death Benefit Planning

Bundled life insurance is a type of insurance product that combines multiple types of insurance coverage into one policy. It is commonly used for death benefit planning purposes. The life insurance coverage offered in a bundled policy often includes term life, whole life, and/or universal life insurance. By bundling multiple types of insurance, a policyholder can save money on premiums and streamline their insurance coverage. Additionally, the death benefit of a bundled life insurance policy can be used to help support the policyholder's beneficiaries in the event of their death, making it an important tool for estate planning.

2.10. Example of a Bundled Life Insurance Plan

A bundled life insurance plan is a package of insurance products offered by an insurance company that combines various types of life insurance coverage. For example, a common type of bundled insurance plan combines a life insurance policy with a long-term care insurance policy. The life insurance policy provides a death benefit for the policyholder's beneficiaries, while the long-term care insurance policy provides financial coverage for the policyholder if they need long-term care.

Another example of a bundled life insurance plan is a term life insurance policy combined with a critical illness insurance policy. The term life insurance policy provides death benefit coverage, while the critical illness insurance policy provides financial coverage if the policyholder is diagnosed with a critical illness. These two policies are bundled together to offer the policyholder comprehensive coverage in the event of death or critical illness.

2.11. Specific Example and Formula for Calculating the Benefit of a Bundled Life Insurance Plan

The benefit of a bundled life insurance plan depends on several factors, such as the policyholder's age, health, coverage amount, policy term, and the insurance company's pricing. There is no specific formula for calculating the benefit of a bundled life insurance plan, as it can vary from person to person and policy to policy.

Typically, a bundled life insurance plan combines several types of insurance policies such as life insurance, long-term care insurance, and/or annuity products into a single package. The main advantage of a bundled life insurance plan is that it can provide comprehensive coverage and can be more cost-effective than purchasing separate policies.

To determine the specific benefit of a bundled life insurance plan, a financial advisor or insurance agent will need to evaluate the policyholder's individual needs and circumstances. They can then provide a personalized quote and discuss the details of the coverage, including any limitations or exclusions.

2.12. How to Use Cash Value Life Insurance to Stockpile Wealth

Cash value life insurance can be used to build wealth through the accumulation of cash value over time. The policyholder pays premiums, which are partially invested and partially used to provide coverage in the event of death. Over time, the policy's cash value can grow and become an available resource for the policyholder. Some policies also offer riders, such as long-term care riders, that allow the policyholder to access the cash value for other purposes, such as to pay for long-term care expenses.

However, it is important to note that life insurance is generally not considered an investment and may not offer the same returns as other investment products. Additionally, there are often restrictions on accessing the cash value and potential tax implications to consider. Before using life insurance to stockpile wealth, consult with a financial advisor to evaluate your overall financial goals and risk tolerance.

Example of Using Cash Value Life Insurance to Build Wealth

Cash value life insurance is a type of permanent life insurance that can be used to build wealth by allowing the policyholder to accumulate cash value over time. The cash value can be invested in various financial products and used as collateral to take out loans. To use cash-value life insurance to build wealth, the policyholder must pay higher premiums than they would with term life insurance. The premium payments not only pay for the life insurance coverage but also contribute to the cash value growth.

A whole life insurance policy is one example of using cash-value life insurance to build wealth. The policyholder would pay higher premiums into the policy, which would accumulate cash value over time. The policyholder could then use the accumulated cash value as collateral to take out a loan or to invest in other financial products. If the policyholder dies, the death benefit from the life insurance policy would go to their beneficiaries tax-free.

It is important to note that using life insurance as an investment strategy is not suitable for everyone, and it's important to consider the costs and risks involved. It's advisable to consult a financial advisor before making any investment decisions.

Chapter 3
Alternative Investments

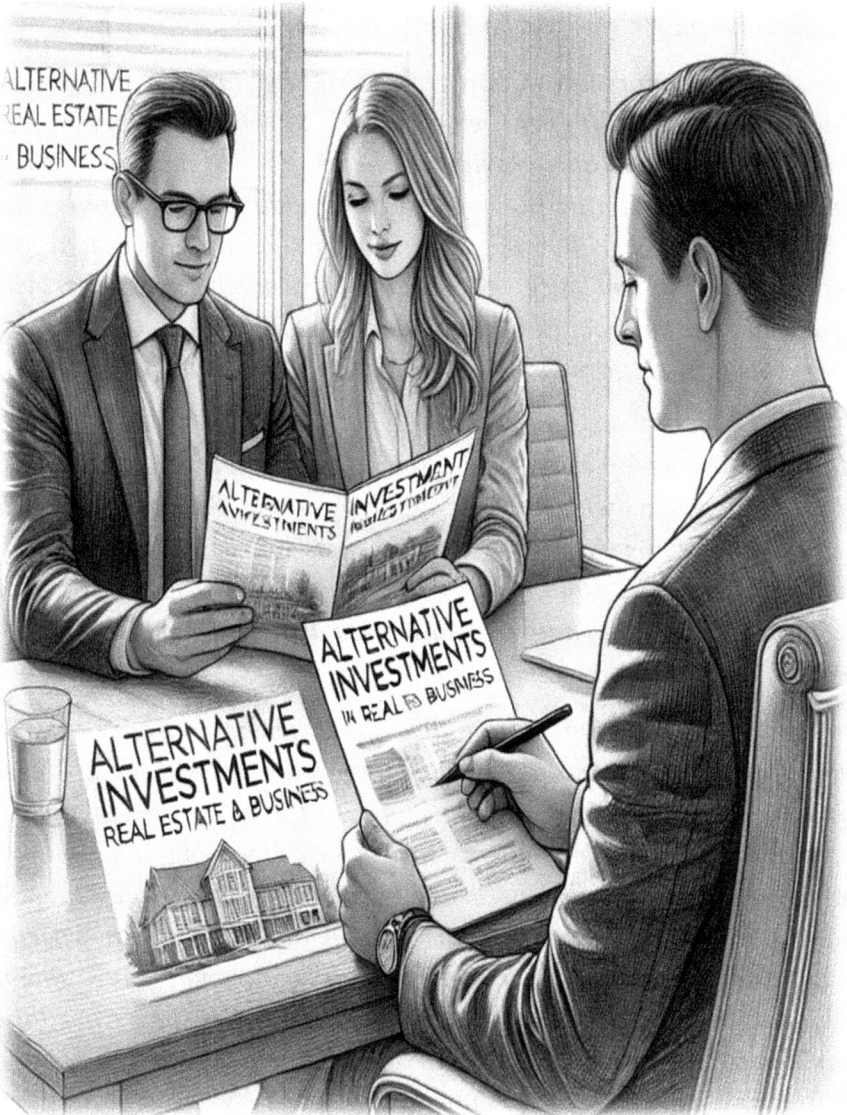

Understanding alternative investments is increasingly important for investors seeking to diversify their portfolios and potentially enhance returns beyond traditional stocks and bonds. Alternative investments encompass a wide range of asset classes and strategies that are not part of conventional investment categories. This includes private equity, hedge funds, real estate, commodities, and tangible assets like art and antiques.

One of the primary attractions of alternative investments is their potential to offer higher returns and lower correlations with traditional markets, thus providing a hedge against market volatility and inflation. Additionally, they can bring unique opportunities and risks, requiring a different approach to due diligence and risk assessment. For instance, real estate investments might provide steady income and capital appreciation, while private equity could offer substantial growth potential through investments in private companies.

However, the complexity and often opaque nature of alternative investments make them challenging for investors. They typically have higher minimum investment requirements, longer lock-up periods, and less liquidity than traditional investments. Moreover, the performance of alternative investments can be more difficult to predict, and they often involve higher fees.

Investors considering alternative investments need a solid understanding of these factors and how they fit into their overall investment strategy and risk tolerance. Having a well-diversified portfolio is usually recommended before allocating a significant portion to alternatives. Due to the specialized knowledge required, many investors seek the guidance of financial advisors with expertise in alternative investments. In summary, while alternative investments can be a valuable component of a sophisticated investment portfolio, they demand careful consideration and an in-depth understanding of their unique characteristics and risks.

3.1. Introduction to Alternative Investments

Alternative investments are assets that diverge from traditional investments like stocks, bonds, and cash. They are typically less liquid and can encompass a wide range of options, from real estate and private equity to commodities and hedge funds. Alternative investments offer unique opportunities for diversification, risk management, and potentially higher returns.

3.2. What Is an Alternative Investment?

An alternative investment is a type of investment that is not a traditional investment, such as stocks, bonds, and cash. Alternative investments include assets that are not publicly traded on a stock exchange and may be less liquid, more complex, or more volatile than traditional investments.

Alternative investments include a wide variety of assets, such as:

Real estate: Investment in commercial or residential properties or real estate investment trusts (REITs)

Private equity: Investment in private companies or venture capital funds

Hedge funds: Investment in a fund that uses a wide range of strategies to generate returns, such as short selling or leveraging.

Commodities: Investment in natural resources such as gold, oil, or agricultural products.

Art, antiques, and other collectibles

Cryptocurrencies

Infrastructure: Investment in energy, transportation, or communication infrastructure projects

Alternative investments tend to have higher returns and higher risk than traditional investments. They are often used to diversify an investment portfolio and generate returns that are not correlated with those of traditional investments.

It's important to note that alternative investments can be more complex and less transparent than traditional investments, and they may have higher fees and expenses. They also might be less regulated and may not be suitable for all investors. It's always best to consult with a financial advisor or professional to determine if alternative investments are suitable for your circumstances and financial goals and to understand the potential risks and benefits of alternative investments.

3.3. Qualifications for Investors in an Alternative Investment

Alternative investments are not suitable for all investors, as they can be more complex, less transparent, and have higher risks than traditional investments. To be eligible to invest in alternative investments, investors typically need to meet certain qualifications. These qualifications can vary depending on the type of alternative investment, but they generally include:

- **Accreditation**: Some alternative investments, such as private equity and hedge funds, are only available to accredited investors. To be an accredited investor, an individual must have a net worth of at least $1 million, not including their primary residence, or have had an income of at least $200,000 per year ($300,000 for married couples) for the past two years and expect to have that income again in the current year.
- **Minimum investment amount**: Many alternative investments require a minimum investment of $10,000 or more, which can make them less accessible to small investors.
- **Experience and sophistication**: Alternative investments can be more complex and less transparent than traditional investments, and they may require a higher level of investment knowledge and experience. As a result, many alternative

investment opportunities are only available to investors with a certain level of investment experience and sophistication.

- **Risk tolerance**: Alternative investments tend to be riskier and more volatile than traditional investments. Investors should have a high-risk tolerance and be prepared to lose some or all of their investments.

Investing in alternatives is often subject to certain qualifications and regulations, primarily to protect less experienced investors. These qualifications may include:

- **Accredited Investor Status**: Many alternative investments are limited to accredited investors, individuals, or entities with a certain level of income or net worth.
- **Sophisticated Investor Status**: Some alternative investments may be accessible to investors who meet specific knowledge or experience criteria.
- **Minimum Investment Requirements**: Many alternative investments have high minimum investment thresholds, which can be a barrier for some investors.

It's important to note that the qualifications for investing in alternative investments can vary depending on the type of investment, the jurisdiction, and the individual's circumstances. It's always best to consult with a financial advisor or professional to understand the qualifications required for alternative investments and determine if they suit your circumstances and financial goals.

3.4. Types of Alternative Investments

Alternative investments encompass a broad spectrum of options:

- **Private Equity**: Private equity involves investing in private companies, often through venture capital or buyouts. Investors may acquire equity in a private company to improve its performance and sell it at a profit.

- **Real Estate**: Real estate investments include buying physical properties, real estate investment trusts (REITs), and real estate crowdfunding platforms. Real estate offers the potential for rental income and property appreciation.
- **Commodities**: Investing in commodities involves buying physical goods like gold, oil, or agricultural products. These investments can provide diversification and serve as hedges against inflation.
- **Hedge Funds**: Hedge funds are actively managed investment pools that employ various strategies to generate returns. They may use leverage, short selling, and derivatives to achieve their goals.
- **Private Debt**: Private debt investments involve lending money to companies or individuals outside of traditional banking channels. These investments can offer higher interest rates but carry credit risk.
- **Venture Capital**: Venture capital investments fund early-stage startups in exchange for equity. Investors hope to profit from the companies' growth and eventual exits through IPOs or acquisitions.
- **Collectibles**: Collectibles like art, rare coins, and vintage cars can appreciate over time. Investing in collectibles requires expertise and a passion for the chosen niche.
- **Infrastructure**: Infrastructure investments fund essential public projects like bridges, roads, and utilities. They often offer stable cash flows and long-term income potential.

3.5. Advantages of Alternative Investments

Investors turn to alternative investments for several advantages:

- **Diversification**: Alternatives can help reduce portfolio risk by providing a low correlation with traditional assets.
- **Potential for Higher Returns**: Some alternatives have the potential for greater returns than traditional investments.

- **Inflation Hedge**: Assets like commodities and real estate can serve as hedges against inflation.
- **Portfolio Risk Management**: Alternatives can be used strategically to manage overall portfolio risk.

3.6. Risks and Challenges of Alternative Investments

While alternative investments offer unique benefits, they also come with risks and challenges:

- **Lack of Liquidity**: Many alternative investments are less liquid than stocks and bonds, making it difficult to access funds quickly.
- **Complexity**: Some alternatives, such as hedge funds and private equity, can be complex and may require a deep understanding of the investment strategy.
- **Higher Fees**: Alternative investments often have higher fees and expenses compared to traditional investments.
- **Regulatory Compliance**: Compliance with regulations can be more complex for some alternative investments, particularly for accredited investors.
- **Market Risk**: Depending on the type of alternative, investors may face market risk, credit risk, or other specific risks associated with that asset class.

3.7. Due Diligence in Alternative Investments

Investors considering alternative investments should conduct thorough due diligence. This process involves:

- **Assessing Risk Tolerance**: Determine how much risk you are willing to take with alternative investments.
- **Research Investment Options**: Investigate specific alternatives, their historical performance, and their suitability for your goals.

- **Understanding Fees**: Be aware of all fees and expenses associated with the investment.
- **Evaluating the Manager**: If applicable, assess the investment manager or fund's track record and expertise.
- **Diversification**: Consider how the alternative investment fits into your overall portfolio and strategy.
- **Exit Strategy**: Understand how and when you can exit the investment if needed.

3.8. Adding Alternatives to a Portfolio

Alternative investments should be integrated strategically into a portfolio. This involves:

- **Asset Allocation**: Based on your risk tolerance and goals, determine the percentage of your portfolio allocated to alternatives.
- **Portfolio Diversification**: Ensure that adding alternatives enhances overall portfolio diversification.
- **Monitoring**: Continuously monitor the performance of alternative investments and their impact on the portfolio.
- **Rebalancing**: Periodically rebalance the portfolio to maintain the desired asset allocation.

3.9. Conclusion

Alternative investments offer opportunities for diversification and potentially higher returns, but they also come with unique risks and complexities. Investors should carefully evaluate these investments and consider their suitability within their broader financial goals and risk tolerance.

3.10. Additional Resources

Consider consulting with a financial advisor or investment professional experienced in alternative investments for personalized guidance. Additionally, being informed about the latest developments in the alternative investment landscape is essential for making informed decisions in this evolving field.

Chapter 4
Professional Advice

Understanding the importance of receiving financial advice is crucial for investors at all experience levels. Navigating the complex world of investments, retirement planning, tax strategies, and wealth management can be daunting. Professional financial advice is pivotal in helping investors make informed decisions, align financial strategies with their goals, and manage risks effectively.

The landscape of financial advice is diverse, ranging from comprehensive financial planning to specific investment recommendations or tax advice. A key aspect for investors is recognizing their limitations regarding expertise, time, and resources for managing their finances. Financial advisors bring a wealth of knowledge and experience, offering insights that can help identify opportunities and avoid common pitfalls.

Professional advice is particularly valuable in developing a holistic financial plan encompassing various elements like asset allocation, retirement planning, estate planning, and risk management. This advice can be tailored to individual needs, whether it's for a young professional starting to build wealth or for someone approaching retirement.

However, investors should also be discerning when choosing a financial advisor. Critical considerations include credentials, experience, the advisor's fee structure (fee-only or commission-based), and the advisor's fiduciary responsibility to act in the client's best interest. Moreover, effective communication and a clear understanding of the investor's goals, risk tolerance, and financial situation are essential for a successful advisor-investor relationship.

Seeking financial advice involves delegating financial decisions and empowering oneself through professional guidance and expertise.

4.1. Due Diligence When Choosing a Financial Advisor

Due diligence is a critical process when selecting a financial advisor, as it involves thoroughly evaluating and vetting the individual to ensure they are trustworthy, competent, and a good fit for your financial needs and goals.

Rationale for Why Due Diligence Is Necessary:

- **Assessing Qualifications and Experience**: It's important to confirm that the financial advisor has the necessary qualifications, including certifications (such as a CFP or CFA) and relevant experience. This helps ensure that they have the expertise to provide sound advice.
- **Understanding the Advisor's Approach**: Due diligence helps you understand the advisor's strategies and whether they align with your risk tolerance, investment philosophy, and long-term objectives.
- **Evaluating Track Record**: Investigating the advisor's past performance and the outcomes they have achieved for other clients can provide insights into their effectiveness and reliability.
- **Identifying Conflicts of Interest**: Identifying any potential conflicts of interest the advisor may have, such as receiving commissions for selling certain products, is crucial. A fiduciary, for instance, is legally obligated to act in your best interest.
- **Reviewing Regulatory Compliance and History**: For your financial safety, check if the advisor has had any disciplinary action or complaints against them and ensure they are compliant with financial regulations.
- **Understanding Fees and Compensation**: Knowing how the advisor is compensated (fee-only, commission-based, etc.) is important to avoid hidden costs and ensure their compensation structure does not influence their advice.

- **Personal Compatibility**: You must feel comfortable with your advisor on a personal level, as a good working relationship is key to effective financial planning.
- **Checking References and Reviews**: Speaking with current or past clients and reading reviews and testimonials can provide additional insights into the advisor's reliability and quality of service.
- **Security and Privacy**: Ensure that your financial advisor has robust measures to protect your personal and financial information.
- **Regular Monitoring and Evaluation**: Due diligence is not a one-time process. Reviewing and evaluating your advisor's performance regularly is important to ensure they continue to meet your financial needs and adhere to professional standards.

When choosing a financial advisor, due diligence is essential for protecting your investments, ensuring professional and ethical service, and finding a match that suits your financial goals and personal preferences.

4.2. Building an Investment Portfolio Spreadsheet

Building an investment portfolio spreadsheet is an essential step in managing your investments effectively. The spreadsheet should include the following components:

- **Asset Allocation**: Define the percentage of your portfolio allocated to different asset classes, such as stocks, bonds, and alternative investments.
- **Investment Selection**: List the specific investments within each asset class, including individual stocks, bonds, mutual funds, or exchange-traded funds (ETFs).
- **Current Holdings**: Track the quantity and current value of each investment in your portfolio.

- **Purchase Price**: Record the price at which you acquired each investment.
- **Market Value**: Continuously update the market value of each investment to monitor portfolio performance.
- **Income and Dividends**: Track any income or dividends your investments generate.
- **Performance Metrics**: To assess investment performance, include metrics like return on investment (ROI) and annualized returns.
- **Risk Assessment**: Evaluate the risk associated with each investment, considering factors like volatility and correlation.
- **Rebalancing**: Set triggers for rebalancing your portfolio to maintain your desired asset allocation.

4.3. How to Find a Financial Advisor

Finding a financial advisor is critical in managing your investments and achieving your financial goals. Consider the following steps when searching for a financial advisor:

- **Identify Your Needs**: Determine your specific financial needs, whether retirement planning, investment management, estate planning, or a combination of services.
- **Credentials and Qualifications**: Look for advisors with relevant certifications, such as Certified Financial Planner (CFP) or Chartered Financial Analyst (CFA). These designations indicate a commitment to professionalism and knowledge.
- **Referrals**: Seek recommendations from trusted friends, family members, or colleagues who have had positive experiences with financial advisors.
- **Interview Multiple Advisors**: Consult with multiple advisors to assess their expertise, communication style, and fees.

- **Look for Transparency**: Work with advisors who are transparent about their fees and services and explain their investment strategies clearly.
- **Assess Compatibility**: Meet with potential advisors to assess their communication style, investment philosophy, and overall approach to client collaboration. Ensure you feel comfortable with the advisor and believe they will have your best interests in mind.
- **Ensure Proper Licensing**: Verify that the advisor is licensed and authorized to sell financial products and services in your state.
- **Check Their Background**: You can check their background and see if they have any disclosures or complaints via FINRA's BrokerCheck.
- **Consider Fee Structure**: Consider their fee structure, whether fee-only, commission-based, or a mix of both.

It is also important to work with an advisor who can help you understand the complex and ever-changing financial market. They should be able to explain the diverse types of financial products and services, their benefits and drawbacks, and how they align with your personal goals and risk tolerance.

It's always best to consult with a financial advisor or professional to understand each option's potential benefits and drawbacks and determine if they suit your circumstances and financial goals.

- **Fiduciary vs. Broker**: Understand the difference between fiduciary advisors (who are legally obligated to act in your best interest) and brokers (who may have conflicting interests).
- **Background Check**: Research an advisor's background, including any disciplinary history or customer complaints.

4.4. Why Hire a Fiduciary vs. a Broker?

Choosing between a fiduciary and a broker is a critical decision when seeking financial advice. Hiring a fiduciary over a broker can offer several advantages, including:

- **Legal Obligation**: A fiduciary is legally obligated to act in the best interests of their clients. They must prioritize their clients' interests over their own, and their recommendations must be based on the client's best interests, not on what generates the most commission or fees for themselves.
- **Transparency**: Fiduciaries are required to disclose all fees and conflicts of interest and provide their clients with complete transparency regarding their investment strategy, potential risks, and expected returns.
- **Customized Advice**: A fiduciary takes the time to understand their client's financial goals, risk tolerance, and investment preferences to develop a customized investment plan that meets their specific needs.
- **Lower Costs**: Fiduciaries are typically fee-only, meaning they charge a flat fee or a percentage of assets under management rather than commissions on trades or sales. Over time, this can lead to lower costs for clients.

Conversely, brokers typically work on commission and may prioritize their monetary interests over their clients. They may not have a legal obligation to act in their client's best interests, and their recommendations may not always suit their clients' needs.

Hiring a fiduciary or a broker will ultimately depend on your needs and preferences. A fiduciary may be a better choice if you seek a trusted advisor who puts your interests first and provides transparent, customized advice.

4.5. Should I Work with a Fiduciary or Broker with My Retirement Funds?

A fiduciary must act in your best interests and provide advice tailored to your financial situation and goals.

Regarding retirement planning, a fiduciary can help you create a personalized plan that considers age, income, retirement goals, and risk tolerance. They can also provide ongoing guidance and support, allowing you to adjust your investment strategy as circumstances change.

In contrast, brokers often receive commissions for recommending certain investments, which can create conflicts of interest and may not always be in your best interests. Additionally, brokers may not be required to provide the same level of transparency and disclosure as fiduciaries.

Ultimately, deciding whether to work with a fiduciary or a broker will depend on your needs and circumstances. However, suppose you are looking for a trusted advisor who is legally obligated to act in your best interests and provide personalized advice. In that case, a fiduciary is generally the better choice for managing your retirement funds.

4.6. How to Tell if a Financial Advisor Is More Interested in Commission Than Proper Advice

It can be difficult to tell if a financial advisor is more interested in earning commission than providing proper advice. However, there are red flags that may indicate that an advisor is more interested in their financial gain than in the best interests of their clients:

- **High-Pressure Sales Tactics**: Advisors who use high-pressure sales tactics to push products or services may focus more on earning commissions than providing proper advice.
- **Limited Product Offerings**: Advisors who only offer a limited range of products or services may be more interested in earning commissions from those products than in providing a diverse range of options that align with the client's goals and risk tolerance.

- **Lack of Transparency**: Advisors who are not transparent about their fees, services, or investment strategies may be more focused on earning commissions than providing proper advice.
- **Unsuitable Recommendations**: Advisors who recommend products or services unsuitable for the client's goals, risk tolerance, or overall financial situation may be more focused on earning commissions than providing proper advice.
- **Not Licensed**: Advisors who are not licensed to sell financial products or services in your state or who have a history of regulatory actions may be more focused on earning commissions than providing proper advice.

It's important to remember that not all advisors who earn commissions are necessarily more interested in their own financial gain than in the best interests of their clients. However, it's always best to be aware of these red flags and work with a financial advisor or professional aligning with your circumstances and financial goals.

4.7. Choosing Between a Large Financial Advisory Firm and a Small Independent Advisor

Choosing between a large financial advisory firm and a small independent advisor involves weighing various factors:

Large Financial Advisory Firm

- **Resource Availability:** Large firms often have more resources, including research, tools, and technology.
- **Diverse Expertise:** They usually have teams with diverse expertise in different financial areas.
- **Brand Stability:** Large firms may offer more stability and a sense of security due to their established presence.
- **Wide Range of Services:** They might provide a broader range of services, from investment management to estate planning.

- **Global Presence:** Beneficial for clients with international financial needs or investments.

Small Independent Advisor

- **Personalized Service:** Small advisors often offer more personalized and tailored advice.
- **Flexibility:** Independent advisors might be more flexible and responsive to individual client needs.
- **Lower Costs:** Due to lower overhead costs, independent advisors may have lower fees than larger firms.
- **Less Bias:** They might have fewer conflicts of interest and can offer more unbiased advice.
- **Stronger Relationships:** Typically, you'll have direct access to the advisor, fostering a more personal relationship.

Ultimately, the choice depends on your specific financial needs, preferences for personalized service, and comfort level with the advisory entity's size and scope.

4.8. Always Ask a Financial Advisor About the Overall Costs of Management

The best way to ask a financial advisor about the overall costs of management is to be direct and specific in your question. You can ask the advisor to provide a detailed breakdown of all the fees and expenses associated with managing your portfolio. This includes any upfront fees, ongoing management fees, transaction fees, and any other applicable charges.

Key Costs to Inquire About:

- **Management Fees:** Fees charged by the advisor for managing your investments.
- **Expense Ratios:** Fees associated with mutual funds or ETFs within your portfolio.

- **Trading Costs:** Expenses related to buying and selling securities.
- **Advisory Fees:** Charges for financial planning and advisory services.
- **Hidden Costs:** Be aware of any hidden fees or charges, such as transaction fees or tax implications of portfolio turnover.

It's also important to ask about hidden costs or charges that may not be immediately apparent. Additionally, you may want to ask about the advisor's fee structure, such as whether they charge a flat fee or a percentage of assets under management. Understanding the costs associated with management is important so you can make an informed decision about whether the advisor's services align with your investment goals and budget.

4.9. Can You Test a Financial Advisor to Ensure They Have Your Best Interests When Advising You?

There are several ways to test a financial advisor to ensure they have your best interests in mind when advising you.

Key Steps to Evaluate a Financial Advisor:

- **Check Credentials and Qualifications**: Verify the advisor's qualifications and experience. Use FINRA's BrokerCheck or the SEC's Investment Adviser Public Disclosure (IAPD) to review their professional background, licenses, and any past disciplinary actions.
- **Ask About Their Investment Philosophy**: Inquire about their investment approach and strategy. Ensure their approach aligns with your financial goals and risk tolerance.
- **Ask About Fees and Compensation**: A fiduciary advisor, who is legally required to act in the best interest of their clients, will be transparent about their fees. Ask for a clear breakdown of all fees and how the advisor is compensated.

- **Request a Written Investment Plan**: Request a formal investment plan to see how the advisor intends to help you achieve your goals. This will also provide a clear framework for tracking progress.
- **Ask for References**: Speak with current or previous clients to learn about their experiences with the advisor.
- **Inquire About Fiduciary Status**: Confirm if the advisor is legally bound by fiduciary duty to act in your best interest.
- **Check for Conflicts of Interest**: Ask about any potential conflicts of interest, such as commission-based compensation or affiliations with specific financial institutions.
- **Stay Informed**: Continuously educate yourself about financial matters to better evaluate the advice you receive.

4.10. Build a Current Investment Request for Proposal (RFP) to Present to Potential Financial Advisors

An RFP (Request for Proposal) is a document that outlines your investment goals, objectives, and requirements for a financial advisor. It is used to solicit proposals from potential advisors and to compare their qualifications, fees, and services.

Steps to Build a Current Investment RFP:

- **Introduction**: Provide background information about your financial situation and goals.
- **Scope of Services**: Clearly outline the services you expect from the advisor, whether investment management, financial planning, or both.
- **Define Your Investment Goals and Objectives**: Clearly state your investment goals and objectives, such as growth, income, or capital preservation.
- **Identify Your Investment Time Horizon**: Specify how long you plan to invest, whether short-term, medium-term, or long-term.

- **Outline Your Risk Tolerance**: Describe your risk tolerance, such as conservative, moderate, or aggressive.
- **Describe Your Investment Experience**: Share information about your investment experience, including any previous investments you've made.
- **Provide Information About Your Current Portfolio**: Include details about your current portfolio, such as the types of assets you hold, their value, and their performance.
- **Specify Your Fee Structure**: Clearly state the fee structure you prefer, such as a flat fee, a percentage of assets under management, or a combination of both.
- **Request Information About the Advisor's Qualifications**: Ask for details on the advisor's education, experience, and professional designations.
- **Request References**: Ask for references from the advisor's current or former clients.
- **Request a Sample Portfolio**: Ask for a sample portfolio that aligns with your investment goals and objectives.
- **Include a Date for Proposal Submission**: Specify a deadline for the advisor to submit their proposal.
- **Conflict of Interest Disclosure**: Ask the advisor to disclose any potential conflicts of interest.
- **Compliance and Regulation**: Ensure the advisor is in compliance with industry regulations.

Conducting a Background Check on a Financial Advisor

Conducting a thorough background check on a financial advisor is crucial to ensure their credibility and trustworthiness.

Here's a step-by-step guide:

1. Check Credentials and Registrations:

- Verify their credentials (like CFP, CFA) through the issuing organizations (e.g., CFP Board for Certified Financial Planners).
- Ensure they are registered with the proper authorities, such as the SEC (for Registered Investment Advisors) or FINRA (for broker-dealers).
- Use FINRA's BrokerCheck or the SEC's Investment Adviser Public Disclosure website to verify registration.

2. Review Employment History:
   - Look into their employment history for stability and relevant experience.
   - Check their LinkedIn profile or ask for a resume.

3. Check for Disciplinary Actions and Legal Issues:
   - Use FINRA's BrokerCheck or the SEC's IAPD to see if they have any disciplinary actions or legal issues in their history.

4. Read Client Reviews and Testimonials:
   - Read reviews to get insights into the advisor's service quality and client satisfaction. Be cautious of overly positive or negative reviews.

5. Interview the Advisor:
   - Ask about their experience, investment philosophy, and how they handle client relationships.
   - Pay attention to their communication style and whether they seem to understand your financial goals.

6. Request References:
   - Ask for references from current or past clients to hear firsthand experiences.

7. Review Their Fee Structure:
   - Understand how they are compensated (e.g., flat fee, percentage of assets under management, or commissions).
   - Look for any potential conflicts of interest related to their compensation model.

8. Check for Fiduciary Duty:

- Determine if they are a fiduciary, which means they are legally required to act in your best interest.
9. Assess Their Communication and Service Level:
   - Ensure their communication style and service level meet your expectations.
10. Conduct a Deeper Background Check:
   - Consider using a professional background check service to uncover any criminal records, bankruptcy filings, or other red flags.

A good financial advisor should be transparent about their qualifications, history, and how they can assist with your financial goals. Trust your instinct; if something feels off, it's worth doing additional research.

Note: Financial advisors have different strategies and fee structures. Before you start building your RFP, clearly understand your investment goals and risk tolerance. Reviewing the proposal with a legal or financial expert is wise to ensure it's in your best interest.

4.11. What to Do If You Feel That You Were Treated Unfairly by an Advisor

If you feel that you were treated unfairly by a financial advisor, there are several steps you can take to address the issue:

- **Document the Problem**: Keep detailed records of all correspondence, statements, and other documentation related to the issue. Include the advisor's name, contact information, and the date of the incident.
- **Contact the Advisor**: Try to resolve the problem by speaking directly with the advisor. Explain the issue and provide any relevant documentation. If the advisor is unwilling or unable to resolve the issue, ask to talk with their supervisor or manager.

- **File a Complaint**: If you cannot resolve the issue directly with the advisor, file a complaint with the advisor's firm or the regulatory agency that oversees the advisor's activities.
- **File a Complaint with FINRA**: If the advisor is a registered representative, you can file a complaint with the Financial Industry Regulatory Authority (FINRA). Complaints can be filed online, by mail, or by phone.
- **Seek Legal Action**: If the issue cannot be resolved through other means, you may consider seeking legal action. It's important to consult with an attorney to understand the potential benefits and drawbacks of legal action and determine if it is the right course of action for your circumstances.

It's important to remember that resolving a complaint may take time, and it may not always result in a favorable outcome. However, addressing the issue can help protect your interests and hold the advisor accountable for their actions.

4.12. Conclusion

Seeking professional financial advice is a critical step in achieving your financial goals. Whether you choose a fiduciary or a broker, it's essential to conduct due diligence, ask relevant questions, and ensure that the advisor's interests align with your financial well-being. A well-informed and transparent advisor can significantly influence your financial success.

Chapter 5
Investment Options

For investors, understanding the array of investment options available is fundamental to successful financial planning and wealth building. The investment landscape offers diverse possibilities, each with its own risk-reward profile, including stocks, bonds, mutual funds, exchange-traded funds (ETFs), real estate, and increasingly popular alternative investments like cryptocurrencies and commodities.

The first step for any investor is to clarify their financial goals, investment horizon, and risk tolerance. Different investment vehicles serve different purposes: stocks offer growth potential but come with higher volatility, and bonds provide income and stability. Still, they might offer lower returns, while mutual funds and ETFs offer diversification and professional management. Real estate can provide tangible assets and potential rental income, whereas alternative investments offer higher returns and diversification but often have higher risks and less liquidity.

Understanding these options is critical for potential returns and managing risk through diversification. A well-balanced investment portfolio tailored to an individual's goals can help mitigate risks and smooth out the volatility inherent in financial markets. This is particularly important in changing economic environments, where different asset classes can react differently to market forces.

Moreover, investors must know the costs of different investment options, including management fees, transaction costs, and tax implications. These costs can significantly impact net returns.

Gaining a comprehensive understanding of the various investment options is essential for any investor. It enables informed decision-making, aligns investments with personal financial goals, and helps navigate the complexities of the financial markets. For many, this pursuit often involves seeking advice from financial professionals to gain deeper insights and personalized strategies.

5.1. Introduction to Investment Options

Investment options encompass a wide range of financial instruments and assets that individuals and institutions can use to grow their wealth. These options provide different opportunities for generating returns, managing risk, and achieving various financial goals.

5.2. Dollar Cost Averaging (DCA)

Dollar Cost Averaging (DCA) is an investment strategy that consistently invests a fixed dollar amount at regular intervals, regardless of market conditions. The idea behind DCA is that by investing a fixed amount of money at regular intervals, an investor can reduce the risk of investing a large sum of money at the wrong time, such as when the market is at a peak.

DCA has several advantages:

Risk Mitigation: DCA spreads the investment over time, reducing the impact of market volatility.

Disciplined Investing: It encourages disciplined investing by automating contributions.

Potential for Lower Average Costs: DCA may result in a lower average purchase price of assets over time.

How it works:

An investor decides on a fixed amount of money to invest each month, regardless of market conditions.

The investor then uses this fixed amount to purchase shares of a particular investment at regular intervals, such as monthly or quarterly.

As the market fluctuates, the investor will purchase more shares when the market is down and fewer shares when the market is up.

The goal of DCA is to reduce the risk of investing a large sum of money at the wrong time and to take advantage of market fluctuations by purchasing more shares when the market is down and fewer when the market is up.

It's important to keep in mind that DCA doesn't guarantee profits, and it doesn't protect against market loss. It's simply a strategy to reduce the risk of buying at the wrong time. Additionally, DCA may not be suitable for all investors, and it's important to consult with a financial advisor or professional to determine if it is the right strategy for your individual circumstances and financial goals.

5.3. Understanding Corporate Bonds

Corporate bonds are debt securities issued by companies to raise capital. They are similar to government bonds, but instead of the government issuing the bonds, they are issued by corporations. When investors buy a corporate bond, they essentially lend money to the company that issued the bond. The company, in turn, promises to pay the investor a fixed interest rate (coupon) and return the principal at the bond's maturity date.

Key concepts related to corporate bonds include:

Credit Quality: Corporate bonds have varying levels of credit risk, ranging from investment-grade to high-yield (junk) bonds.

Yield and Coupon Rate: The yield reflects the return on the bond based on its current price, while the coupon rate is the fixed interest rate specified in the bond's contract.

Maturity: Bonds can have short, intermediate, or long maturities, affecting their sensitivity to interest rate changes.

Corporate bonds have a wide range of maturities, from a few months to 30 years, and they can be issued in various denominations, usually $1,000 or $5,000. They trade in the secondary market, and their prices fluctuate based on supply and demand and the issuer's creditworthiness.

Investing in corporate bonds can provide a steady stream of income and diversification benefits to a portfolio. They also offer higher yields than government bonds but come with higher credit risk. This means that if a company defaults on its debt, bondholders may not recover all or any of their investments.

To assess the credit risk of a particular bond, investors can look at the credit rating assigned to it by credit rating agencies such as Moody's, Standard & Poor's, and Fitch. The higher the credit rating, the lower the credit risk and the higher the price of the bond.

It's important to remember that corporate bonds are subject to interest rate risk. When interest rates rise, the value of existing bonds may fall. Therefore, having a long-term investment horizon and diversifying your bond portfolio by investing in bonds with different maturities and credit ratings is essential.

Consulting with a financial advisor or professional is advisable to understand the potential benefits and drawbacks of investing in corporate bonds and to determine if they align with your overall financial strategy and goals.

5.4. What Does Par Plus Mean When Reviewing the Price of a Corporate Bond

When reviewing the price of a corporate bond, "par plus" means that the bond is trading above its face value or "par" value. A bond's face value, or par value, is the amount it will be worth when it matures. A bond that is trading at par plus means that it is trading at a premium to its face value. For example, a bond with a face value of $1,000 trading at $1,050 is said to be selling at a premium of 5% ($50/$1,000).

When market interest rates fall, bond prices increase, and when they rise, bond prices fall. When a bond's price is trading at a premium, the bond's coupon rate is higher than the current market interest rate, making the bond more attractive to investors.

It's important to note that a bond trading at a premium may not always be a good investment, as it may not provide the same level of return as a bond trading at a discount. Additionally, when a bond is trading at a premium, the investor will receive less interest than the bond's coupon rate because its price is above its face value.

It's always best to consult with a financial advisor or professional to understand the potential benefits and drawbacks of investing in bonds trading at a premium and determine if they suit your circumstances and financial goals.

5.5. What Does a Discount Price of a Corporate Bond Mean

When reviewing the price of a corporate bond, a "discount" means that the bond is trading below its face value or "par" value. A bond's face value, or par value, is the amount it will be worth when it matures. A bond that is trading at a discount means that it is trading below its face value. For example, a bond with a face value of $1,000 trading at $950 is said to be selling at a discount of 5% ($50/$1,000).

When market interest rates rise, bond prices fall, and when they fall, bond prices increase. When a bond's price is trading at a discount, the bond's coupon rate is lower than the current market interest rate, making the bond less attractive to investors.

It's important to note that a bond trading at a discount may not necessarily be a bad investment, as it may provide a higher yield than a bond trading at a premium. Additionally, when a bond trades at a discount, the investor will receive more interest income than the bond's coupon rate because its price is below its face value.

It's always best to consult with a financial advisor or professional to understand the potential benefits and drawbacks of investing in bonds trading at a discount and determine if they suit your circumstances and financial goals. Additionally, it's important to consider the issuer's creditworthiness and the bond's maturity date, as these factors also play a role in the bond's price and potential return.

5.6. Pros and Cons of CD Investment

Certificates of Deposit (CDs) are low-risk, interest-bearing deposits banks and credit unions offer. A certificate of deposit (CD) is a type of savings account that banks and credit unions offer. CDs typically offer a fixed interest rate and a fixed term ranging from a few months to several years.

They have several pros and cons:

Pros:

Safety: CDs are one of the safest investment options. They are insured by the Federal Deposit Insurance Corporation (FDIC) for amounts up to $250,000 per depositor per institution. Your principal deposit is guaranteed, even if the bank fails.

Predictable income: CDs offer a fixed interest rate, which means that the investor knows exactly how much interest they will earn over the term of the CD. This can be helpful for budgeting and planning.

Liquidity: CDs typically have a fixed term, but many banks and credit unions allow investors to withdraw their funds early, usually with a penalty.

Cons:

Low returns: CDs typically offer lower interest rates than other investments, such as stocks or mutual funds.

Lack of flexibility: CDs have a fixed term, and if an investor needs to access their funds before the CD matures, they will usually have to pay a penalty.

Inflation risk: CDs may not keep up with inflation, which means that the purchasing power of the investor's money may decrease over time.

CDs may be a good option for risk-averse investors who are looking for a safe place to park their money and who have a long-term investment horizon. It's always best to consult with a financial advisor or professional to understand the potential benefits and drawbacks of investing in CDs and to determine if they suit your circumstances and financial goals.

5.7. Understanding Municipal Bonds

Municipal bonds, or muni bonds, are debt securities issued by state and local governments, their agencies, and instrumentalities to raise funds for various public projects and services. They are considered a relatively low-risk investment option and are tax-advantaged for certain investors.

Key points to understand about municipal bonds:

Tax-advantaged: Interest from municipal bonds is generally tax-exempt at the federal level and may also be tax-exempt at the state and local level, depending on where the bond is issued and the investor's tax status. This can make them an attractive option for investors in higher tax brackets.

Credit quality: Municipal bonds are rated by rating agencies such as Moody's, S&P, and Fitch, which indicate the issuer's creditworthiness. The higher the rating, the lower the risk of default. However, it's important to note that municipal bonds can still default, although it is less common than corporate bonds.

Maturity and yield: Municipal bonds have a range of maturity dates and can be short-term or long-term. The yield on a municipal bond is the interest rate paid to the bondholder, and it can vary depending on the issuer's creditworthiness, the maturity date, and the current interest rate environment.

Types of municipal bonds: There are different municipal bonds, such as general obligation bonds, revenue bonds, and tax-exempt commercial paper. General obligation bonds are backed by the issuer's full faith and credit, while revenue bonds are backed by the revenue generated by a specific project or facility. Tax-exempt commercial paper is a short-term debt that municipalities issue to raise cash quickly and is considered a low-risk investment.

Investing in municipal bonds: Municipal bonds can be purchased through a broker or financial advisor or a mutual fund or exchange-traded fund (ETF) specializing in municipal bonds.

It's important to remember that municipal bonds are not suitable for everyone. They may not be the best option for those seeking higher returns or those who need access to their money before maturity. It's always best to consult a financial advisor or professional to determine if municipal bonds align with your financial goals and investment strategy.

Chapter 6
Real Estate Investment

Understanding real estate investment is crucial for investors looking to diversify their portfolios and potentially secure a stable source of income. Real estate investment involves purchasing, owning, managing, and selling or renting real estate property for profit. It stands out as a unique asset class with its risks and opportunities.

Real estate can offer several benefits, including the potential for steady cash flow through rental income, appreciation in property value over time, and diversification away from more traditional investments like stocks and bonds. Additionally, it can provide tax advantages through deductions such as mortgage interest, property depreciation, and maintenance expenses.

However, investing in real estate also requires a deep understanding of various factors. These include market dynamics (like location and economic trends), property management, legal issues (such as zoning and tenant laws), and financial considerations (including mortgages, property taxes, and insurance). Real estate investments can be capital-intensive and often require a long-term commitment. They also involve unique risks, such as property market fluctuations, potential vacancies, and the need for ongoing maintenance and management.

Investors should also consider the different types of real estate investments, such as residential, commercial, industrial, and Real Estate Investment Trusts (REITs). Each type comes with its own set of characteristics and risk profiles.

While real estate investment can be a lucrative avenue for wealth generation, it demands thorough research, careful planning, and, often, professional advice. It's suitable for investors willing to commit the time and resources needed to understand and manage these investments effectively.

6.1. Introduction to Real Estate Investment

Real estate investment involves acquiring, owning, and managing properties to generate rental income, capital appreciation, or both. Real estate can be a lucrative and diverse asset class that provides several advantages to investors.

6.2. Real Estate Investment vs. Stock Market Over 20 Years

Real estate and the stock market are long-term investment options, and their performance can vary. Over a 20-year horizon, real estate investment offers several advantages:

Stability: Real estate tends to be less volatile than the stock market, offering stability during economic turbulence.

Income Generation: Rental income from real estate properties can provide a consistent cash flow stream.

Appreciation: Real estate properties may appreciate over time, especially in high-demand areas.

However, real estate investment also has disadvantages, including illiquidity and high upfront costs.

6.3. Understanding Cap Rate

The Capitalization Rate (Cap Rate) is a critical metric in real estate investment. It measures the potential return on investment by dividing the property's net operating income (NOI) by its current market value or acquisition cost. The formula is as follows:

CapRate=NetOperatingIncome(NOI)
PropertyValueCapRate=PropertyValueNetOperatingIncome(NOI)

Higher Cap Rate: Indicates potentially higher returns but may also come with higher risks or lower property values.

Lower Cap Rate: Suggests lower returns but may be associated with lower risk or higher property values.

Investors use cap rates to assess the attractiveness of a real estate investment and compare different properties.

6.4. Reserve Study for Homeowners Association or Condominium

A Reserve Study is a financial planning tool that homeowners' associations (HOAs) or condominium boards use to budget for future maintenance and repair expenses of common areas and shared amenities. The study includes:

Inventory of Common Assets: A list of common property elements and assets that require maintenance.

Assessment of Condition: An evaluation of the current condition of these assets.

Estimated Costs: Estimates of future repair or replacement costs for these assets.

Funding Plan: A plan for allocating funds to cover these costs over time, ensuring that adequate reserves are maintained.

A well-prepared Reserve Study helps HOAs and condominium associations manage their financial responsibilities effectively.

6.5. Why and How Should a Potential Buyer or Investor Request a Copy of a Condominium Reserve Study?

Requesting a copy of the condominium reserve study is most important for potential buyers and investors because it provides valuable insights into the property's financial health and long-term viability. Here's why and how to request it:

Assessment of Financial Health: The study reveals whether the association has set aside sufficient funds to cover future maintenance and repairs, reducing the risk of special assessments on unit owners.

Adequate Planning: Demonstrates the association's commitment to responsible financial planning and management.

To request a copy, contact the HOA or condominium board or ask your real estate agent to facilitate the request.

6.6. How Is a Reserve Study Calculated?

A Reserve Study is typically conducted by a qualified professional or a reserve study specialist. The process involves the following steps:

Asset Inventory: Identify and document all common elements and assets that require maintenance or replacement.

Assessment of Condition: Evaluate each asset's current condition, considering factors like age, wear and tear, and expected lifespan.

Cost Estimation: Estimate the future costs of repairing or replacing each asset based on current market rates and inflation.

Funding Plan: Develop a funding plan that outlines how the association will accumulate and allocate funds to cover these costs over time.

The reserve specialist compiles this information into a comprehensive report for the HOA or condominium board's use in financial planning.

6.7. Example of a Reserve Study Calculation

Suppose a condominium association has identified that the roof of the building needs replacement in 15 years. The estimated cost of the replacement is $200,000. The association wants to ensure sufficient reserves to cover this expense. They calculate:

AnnualContribution=CostofReplacementRemainingUsefulLifeAnnualContribution=RemainingUsefulLifeCostofReplacement

AnnualContribution=$200,00015=$13,333.33AnnualContribution=15$200,000=$13,333.33

So, the association should set aside approximately $13,333.33 annually to fund the roof replacement.

6.8. Hard Money Loans

Hard money loans are a type of short-term, high-interest loan typically used by real estate investors to purchase or renovate investment properties. These loans are typically secured by the property and issued by private individuals or companies rather than traditional banks or financial institutions.

Here are some key points to understand about hard money loans:

Collateral-based: The property typically secures Hard money loans, meaning the lender can foreclose on the property if the borrower defaults.

High-interest rates: Hard money loans typically have higher interest rates than traditional mortgages because they are higher risk. The interest rate can range from 10% to 15%, sometimes even more.

Short-term: Hard money loans are typically short-term, with a 1 to 3 years maturity. They are intended as a temporary solution, not a long-term financing option.

Easy to qualify: Hard money loans are easier to qualify for than traditional loans because the lender is primarily interested in the property's value and not the borrower's creditworthiness.

Used for property investment: Real estate investors use hard money loans to purchase or renovate investment properties. However, they can also be used for other purposes like bridge loans, refinancing, and cash-out refinances.

Risky: Hard money loans are considered more dangerous than traditional loans because the government does not regulate them, and the lender can charge very high interest rates. Additionally, if the property value drops, the borrower may owe more than the property is worth, leaving them in a difficult situation.

It's important to remember that hard money loans are not suitable for everyone. They may not be the best option for those looking for long-term financing or those who want to live in the property. It's always best to consult with a financial advisor or professional to understand the potential benefits and drawbacks of hard money loans and determine if they suit your circumstances and financial goals.

6.9. How to Check an Individual's Credit Risk

When considering a real estate investment involving a borrower, assessing their credit risk is essential. Here are steps to check an individual's credit risk:

Credit Reports: Obtain the borrower's credit report from one or more major credit bureaus (Equifax, Experian, TransUnion). Review the report for any late payments, delinquencies, or derogatory marks.

Credit Score: Check the borrower's credit score, which summarizes their creditworthiness. Higher scores indicate lower credit risk.

Debt-to-Income Ratio: Evaluate the borrower's debt-to-income ratio, which compares their monthly debt payments to their income. A lower ratio is preferable.

Payment History: Review the borrower's payment history on previous loans or mortgages.

Employment and Income Verification: Verify the borrower's employment and income to ensure they have the means to repay the loan.

References: Ask for references from previous landlords or lenders to assess the borrower's reliability.

Background Check: Conduct a background check for any criminal history or legal issues.

6.10. Conclusion

Real estate investment offers diverse opportunities for income generation, capital appreciation, and portfolio diversification. Understanding key concepts like cap rates, reserve studies, and assessing credit risk is crucial for making informed decisions in real estate investments. Thorough due diligence and potentially seeking professional guidance can help investors navigate the complexities of the real estate market effectively.

Chapter 7
Social Security

Comprehending the intricacies of Social Security is a fundamental aspect of retirement planning for investors. Social Security, a government-run program in the United States, provides retirement, disability, and survivor benefits. While it's often considered a safety net for older adults, understanding its nuances is vital for maximizing its benefits as part of a broader retirement strategy.

Firstly, investors need to understand how benefits are calculated. Social Security benefits are based on an individual's earnings history, with the amount adjusted for inflation over their working years. The age at which one receives benefits significantly impacts the monthly payment amount. While individuals can begin receiving benefits as early as age 62, waiting until full retirement age (which varies based on birth year) or even delaying up to age 70 can significantly increase the monthly benefit.

Another key aspect is understanding the implications of working while receiving benefits, especially before retirement age, as this can temporarily reduce the benefit amount. Additionally, investors should be aware of the tax implications of Social Security benefits, as some may be taxable depending on their income level.

Social Security also offers spouse and survivor benefits, which are crucial for retirement planning, especially for couples. These benefits provide financial support to the spouses or children of eligible workers.

A thorough understanding of Social Security is essential for investors to make informed decisions about retirement timing, income planning, and overall financial security. It's often advisable to consult with a financial advisor or utilize Social Security Administration resources for personalized planning based on individual work history and retirement goals.

7.1. Introduction to Social Security

Social Security is a government program in the United States designed to provide financial support to eligible individuals and their families, particularly during retirement or in the event of disability or death. It is one of the country's most significant social welfare programs, established to ensure economic security for citizens.

7.2. Social Security Age 62 vs. Age 66

Social Security benefits are available to eligible individuals as early as age 62, but the age at which you choose to begin receiving benefits significantly affects the amount you receive:

Suppose an individual starts receiving Social Security benefits at age 62, the earliest age at which benefits can be received. In that case, the benefits will be lower than if they wait until their full retirement age (FRA). The FRA for individuals born between 1943 and 1954 is 66, and for those born after that, it gradually increases to 67.

By starting to receive benefits at age 62, an individual will receive a reduced benefit amount, permanently reduced by a certain percentage depending on the year they were born. For example, if an individual's FRA is 66 and they begin receiving benefits at 62, their benefit will be reduced by 30%. For those born in 1960 or later, their benefit will be reduced by 32%.

On the other hand, if the individual delays taking benefits until age 66, when their FRA is reached, they will receive the full benefit amount. If they wait even longer, until age 70, their benefit amount will increase by 8% per year, up to a maximum of 32%.

It's also important to note that waiting to take Social Security benefits until age 70, the latest age at which benefits can be received, can be a good strategy for some people, such as those in good health. However, it may not be the best option for everyone. For example, an individual with a shorter life expectancy may not live long enough to receive the higher benefit amount. It's always best to consult with a financial advisor or professional to understand the benefits and drawbacks of taking Social Security at different ages and determine the best strategy for your circumstances and financial goals.

When to start taking benefits depends on various factors, including your financial needs, health, and longevity expectations.

7.3. Social Security Spouse Benefits

Social Security spouse benefits are a type of benefit available to married individuals who are eligible for Social Security retirement benefits. These benefits are based on the earnings of the spouse who has the higher benefit amount.

Here are some key points to understand about Social Security spouse benefits:

Eligibility: To be eligible for Social Security spouse benefits, the individual must be currently married and at least 62 years old.

Benefit amount: A spouse's benefit equals half of the higher-earning spouse's full retirement benefit amount, determined by their earnings history. The spouse can claim the benefit as early as age 62, but if they claim before reaching the full retirement age (FRA), the benefit amount will be reduced.

Survivor benefits: If one spouse passes away, the surviving spouse may be eligible for survivor benefits. The survivor benefit amount equals the deceased spouse's full retirement benefit if the surviving spouse is at least full retirement age. If not, the benefit is reduced.

Coordination with other benefits: Social Security spouse benefits are coordinated with other benefits for which the individual may be eligible, such as pensions or retirement savings. The Social Security Administration will typically reduce an individual's benefit amount if they also receive benefits from other sources.

Divorce: If a couple gets divorced, the ex-spouse may still be eligible to receive Social Security benefits based on the other spouse's earnings history, as long as the couple was married for at least 10 years and the ex-spouse is not remarried.

It's important to remember that Social Security spouse benefits are complex and unsuitable for everyone. It's always best to consult with a financial advisor or professional to understand the potential benefits and drawbacks of Social Security spouse benefits and determine the best strategy for your circumstances and financial goals.

7.4. Conclusion

Social Security plays a vital role in the financial well-being of millions of Americans. Understanding when to claim benefits, the potential impact of early or delayed claims, and the availability of spousal benefits is essential for optimizing your Social Security benefits and planning for a financially secure retirement. It's advisable to consult with a financial advisor or use online tools provided by the Social Security Administration to make informed decisions about your Social Security benefits.

Chapter 8
401(k) and IRA

Understanding 401(k)s and Individual Retirement Accounts (IRAs) is crucial for investors seeking to secure their financial future, particularly for retirement. These tax-advantaged retirement accounts are cornerstones of personal financial planning in the United States, each offering unique benefits, rules, and limitations.

A 401(k) is an employer-sponsored retirement plan allowing employees to save and invest a portion of their paycheck before taxes are paid. Contributions reduce taxable income, and the investment grows tax-deferred until withdrawal in retirement. Many employers offer a matching contribution up to a certain percentage, essentially free money and a key 401(k) benefit.

On the other hand, IRAs are individual retirement accounts that anyone can open, regardless of their employment status. There are two main types: Traditional IRAs and Roth IRAs. Traditional IRAs offer tax-deferred growth, with taxes paid upon withdrawal, like a 401(k). Roth IRAs are funded with after-tax dollars, allowing for tax-free growth and tax-free withdrawals in retirement, subject to certain conditions.

Investors must understand these accounts' contribution limits, withdrawal rules, and tax implications. For example, early withdrawals can lead to penalties and taxes, and the IRS sets annual contribution limits. The decision between a Roth and a Traditional IRA often hinges on current and expected future tax rates.

Moreover, the investment choices within 401(k)s and IRAs are critical considerations. These can include a range of assets like stocks, bonds, and mutual funds. Investors must align their investment choices with their risk tolerance, investment horizon, and retirement goals.

401(k)s and IRAs are powerful tools for building retirement savings. However, maximizing their benefits requires an understanding of their rules, tax implications, and investment

options. This understanding is vital for creating a solid foundation for retirement planning and ensuring long-term financial security.

8.1. Introduction to 401(k) and IRA

401(k) and Individual Retirement Accounts (IRAs) are tax-advantaged retirement savings vehicles in the United States. They are essential tools for individuals and employees to save and invest for retirement. Each has its own set of rules, benefits, and considerations.

8.2. Mandatory Withdrawal Age for 401(k) and IRA and Amounts That Must Be Withdrawn

401(k) plans and Individual Retirement Accounts (IRAs) are two types of retirement savings plans that have different mandatory ages and rules for required minimum distributions (RMDs).

The mandatory withdrawal age for 401(k) plans is 72, known as the Required Beginning Date (RBD). This means that an individual must begin taking RMDs from their 401(k) plan by April 1 of the year following the year they turn 72. The RMD amount is calculated based on the individual's life expectancy and the account balance as of December 31 of the previous year.

The mandatory withdrawal age for traditional IRAs is also 72. The RBD is April 1 of the year following the year the individual reaches age 72. The RMD amount is calculated using the same method as for 401(k)s, based on the individual's life expectancy and the account balance as of December 31 of the previous year.

A Roth IRA does not have a mandatory withdrawal age, so you can leave the money invested for as long as you like, and no RMD is required.

It's important to note that failure to take the required RMDs can result in a penalty of 50% of the amount that should have been withdrawn, so it's important to be aware of the RMD rules for 401(k)s and IRAs and to plan accordingly.

It's always best to consult with a financial advisor or professional to understand the benefits and drawbacks of the mandatory withdrawal age for 401(k) and IRA and determine the best strategy for your circumstances and financial goals. Failure to take the required withdrawals can result in penalties and additional taxes.

8.3. How to Transfer a 401(k) to an IRA

Transferring a 401(k) to an IRA, often called a rollover, can be done in a few steps:

Open an IRA: Choose a brokerage or financial institution and open an IRA account.

Contact Your 401(k) Provider: Notify your 401(k)-plan administrator about your intention to roll over your funds.

Initiate the Rollover: Request a direct rollover, transferring the funds directly from your 401(k) into your new IRA account. This avoids tax withholding.

Invest Funds: Once the funds are in your IRA, you can choose how to invest them in various assets like stocks, bonds, mutual funds, or other investments.

Review Investments: Regularly review and manage your IRA investments to align with your retirement goals.

8.4. IRA and 401(k) RMD Calculation Example for The RMD Amount, Based on the Individual's Life Expectancy

The Required Minimum Distribution (RMD) amount for a 401(k) or IRA is calculated based on the individual's life expectancy and the account balance as of December 31 of the previous year.

Here is an example of how the RMD amount is calculated:

John is 72 years old and has a 401(k)-account balance of $200,000 as of December 31, 2022. According to the IRS life expectancy tables, John's life expectancy factor is 27.4.

To calculate his RMD, John would divide his account balance of $200,000 by his life expectancy factor of 27.4:

So, John's RMD for the year 2023 is $7,278.

It's important to note that the calculation of the RMD may differ depending on the life expectancy table used by the plan administrator. The calculation is based on life expectancy tables published by the IRS and is subject to change.

It's also important to note that if an individual has multiple IRAs or 401(k)s, RMDs must be calculated separately for each account. Still, the total RMD amount can be taken from one or more of the accounts.

It's always best to consult with a financial advisor or professional to understand the benefits and drawbacks of RMD calculation and determine the best strategy for your circumstances and financial goals.

8.5. Is There Tax Due on Inherited Annuity? When Is Tax Due on an Inherited IRA?

The taxation of inherited annuities and IRAs depends on various factors:

Inherited Annuity: When an individual inherits an annuity, taxes on the account can be due at different times depending on the type of annuity and the beneficiary's relationship to the original contract holder.

Non-Qualified Annuity: The beneficiary will generally have to pay taxes on the withdrawals from the annuity at ordinary income tax rates. The taxes will be based on the withdrawal amount and the beneficiary's individual tax bracket.

Qualified Annuity: Taxes depend on how the original contract holder set up the annuity and whether the contract holder had already begun withdrawing.

Suppose the contract holder has not yet begun taking withdrawals. In that case, the beneficiary will be required to take distributions over their life expectancy, which will be taxed as ordinary income.

Suppose the contract holder has already begun taking withdrawals. In that case, the beneficiary will generally be subject to the same withdrawal rules as the contract holder and taxed as ordinary income.

It's always best to consult with a financial advisor or professional to understand the potential benefits and drawbacks of inheriting an annuity and to determine the best strategy for your circumstances and financial goals. Also, it's important to note that tax laws are subject to change, so you should consult a tax professional for the most up-to-date information.

Notes:

Inherited Annuity: If you inherit an annuity, the taxation depends on whether it's a qualified (pre-tax) or non-qualified (after-tax) annuity. Generally, the earnings portion of a qualified annuity is taxable when withdrawn. Non-qualified annuities may have a different tax treatment.

Inherited IRA: Inherited IRAs have specific rules. If you inherit a traditional IRA, you will typically need to start taking RMDs, and these distributions are subject to income tax. Roth IRAs have different rules, but qualified distributions are typically tax-free.

When is tax due on an inherited IRA?

When an individual inherits an IRA, taxes on the account can be due at different times depending on the type of IRA and the beneficiary's relationship to the original account holder.

Traditional IRA: The beneficiary generally must begin taking Required Minimum Distributions (RMDs) in the year following the original account holder's death. These distributions are taxed as ordinary income. The beneficiary can choose to take the RMDs over their own life expectancy or five years, with the entire balance being withdrawn by the end of the fifth year.

Roth IRA: The beneficiary does not have to take RMDs. They can withdraw the funds over time or all at once, and the withdrawals will be tax-free as long as the account has been open for at least five years.

Inherited IRA: The beneficiary must take RMDs based on the deceased owner's life expectancy, and the distributions are taxable as ordinary income.

It's always best to consult with a financial advisor or professional to understand the potential benefits and drawbacks of inheriting an IRA and to determine the best strategy for your circumstances and financial goals. Additionally, it's important to note that tax laws are subject to change, so you should consult a tax professional for the most up-to-date information.

The tax implications of inherited accounts can vary based on the account type, your relationship to the deceased account owner, and other factors. It's advisable to consult a tax professional for guidance on your specific situation.

8.6. Conclusion

401(k) and IRA accounts are powerful tools for retirement savings, offering tax advantages and flexibility in investment choices. Understanding these accounts' rules, deadlines, and tax implications is crucial for effective retirement planning. It's also recommended to consult with a financial advisor or tax expert to tailor your retirement savings strategy to your individual needs and goals.

Chapter 9
Medicare

Understanding Medicare is essential for effective financial planning and healthcare management for investors, particularly those nearing retirement age. Medicare, a federal health insurance program in the United States, primarily serves individuals aged 65 and older and younger people with certain disabilities. Grasping the intricacies of Medicare helps anticipate healthcare costs and make informed decisions about retirement timing and savings.

Medicare is divided into several parts, each covering different aspects of healthcare:

Part A: *Covers hospital stays, care in a skilled nursing facility, hospice care, and home health care.*

Part B: *Covers certain doctors' services, outpatient care, medical supplies, and preventive services.*

Part D: *Provides prescription drug coverage.*

Additionally, **Medicare Advantage Plans (Part C)** *are offered by private companies approved by Medicare to provide Part A and B benefits, often including drug coverage (Part D).*

Understanding Medicare is crucial for several reasons:

Financial Planning: *Estimating potential healthcare costs in retirement is vital. While Medicare covers many healthcare expenses, it doesn't cover everything (e.g., long-term care, dental, vision, and hearing aids).*

Supplemental Insurance: *Many beneficiaries purchase Medigap, supplemental insurance policies sold by private companies, to cover gaps in original Medicare (Parts A and B).*

Enrollment Deadlines: *Medicare has specific enrollment periods, and missing them can result in penalties and coverage gaps.*

Coverage Choices: Deciding between original Medicare and a Medicare Advantage Plan depends on individual healthcare needs and preferences.

Changing Needs: As health needs evolve, it's important to reevaluate coverage annually, especially during the open enrollment periods.

Investors need to consider how Medicare fits into their broader retirement plan. This includes budgeting for out-of-pocket expenses not covered by Medicare, understanding how Medicare works with other insurance plans, and planning for the potential need for long-term care. Given the complexity of Medicare, many find it beneficial to consult with financial advisors or health insurance specialists to make informed decisions based on their individual health needs and financial situations.

9.1. Introduction to Medicare

Medicare is a federal health insurance program in the United States primarily designed for individuals aged 65 and older. It also covers certain younger individuals with disabilities and those with End-Stage Renal Disease (ESRD). Medicare helps beneficiaries cover medical expenses, including hospital care, medical services, and prescription drugs.

9.2. Explanation of the Four Parts of Medicare

Medicare consists of four main parts, each covering specific healthcare services:

Medicare Part A (Hospital Insurance): Part A covers inpatient hospital care, skilled nursing facility care, hospice care, and home health services. Most beneficiaries do not pay premiums for Part A if they or their spouse paid Medicare taxes while working.

Medicare Part B (Medical Insurance): Part B covers doctor's services, outpatient care, medical supplies, preventive services, and home health services. Beneficiaries pay a monthly premium for Part B.

Medicare Part C (Medicare Advantage): Also known as Medicare Advantage Plans, these are private health insurance plans approved by Medicare. They often combine Part A and Part B coverage and may include additional benefits like prescription drug coverage. Beneficiaries pay premiums to the private insurer offering the plan.

Medicare Part D (Prescription Drug Coverage): Part D covers prescription drugs and is provided through private insurance plans. Beneficiaries choose a Part D plan and pay premiums to the insurer. The coverage helps reduce the cost of prescription medications.

Notes:

Individuals are eligible for Medicare if they are 65 or older and have been legal residents of the United States for at least five years. They can also qualify for Medicare if they have a permanent disability and have been receiving Social Security Disability Insurance (SSDI) for at least two years or if they have ESRD and require regular dialysis or a kidney transplant.

Medicare does not provide complete coverage, and some services and supplies are not covered, such as long-term care, most dental care, and routine vision and hearing exams. Some individuals may purchase additional coverage, such as Medigap or Medicare Advantage plans, to supplement their Medicare coverage.

It's always best to consult with a financial advisor or professional to understand Medicare's potential benefits and drawbacks and determine the best strategy for your circumstances and financial goals.

9.3. Medicare Options for Those Turning 65

When you turn 65 and become eligible for Medicare, you have several options:

Original Medicare (Part A and Part B): You can enroll in Parts A and B to get hospital and medical coverage from the government.

Medicare Advantage (Part C): You can choose a Medicare Advantage plan offered by a private insurer, which typically combines hospital and medical coverage, often with added benefits like prescription drug coverage.

Medicare Part D: If you choose Original Medicare, you can also enroll in a standalone Part D prescription drug plan to get medication coverage.

Medigap: You can purchase a Medigap (Medicare Supplement) policy to help cover out-of-pocket costs like deductibles, copayments, and coinsurance.

Employer Coverage: If you have employer-sponsored health insurance, you may choose to delay Medicare enrollment without facing penalties.

9.4. Medicare Supplement vs. Advantage Plans

Medicare Supplement (Medigap) and Medicare Advantage plans are options for Medicare beneficiaries. Both plans are designed to help beneficiaries pay for costs not covered by Original Medicare.

Medicare Supplement (Medigap) Plans: These private insurance policies help individuals pay for out-of-pocket expenses such as deductibles, copayments, and coinsurance. They are standardized and regulated by the federal government and supplement Original Medicare coverage by filling in the "gaps" in coverage. Medigap plans are only available to individuals enrolled in Original Medicare (Part A and Part B).

Medicare Advantage Plans: Also known as Medicare Part C, private insurance companies offer these plans and provide additional coverage options beyond traditional Medicare. These plans typically include additional benefits such as vision, hearing, dental, and prescription drug coverage. They also include out-of-pocket maximums, which can provide financial protection. Medicare Advantage plans provide an alternative to Original Medicare and typically offer a network of providers that individuals must use.

When comparing Medicare Supplement (Medigap) and Medicare Advantage plans, it's important to consider the individual's needs, budget, and preferred provider network. Medigap plans supplement Original Medicare and have more flexibility in providers, while Advantage plans offer additional benefits but have more restrictive networks. It's always best to consult a financial advisor or professional to determine the best strategy for your circumstances and financial goals.

Notes:

Choosing between a Medicare Supplement (Medigap) plan and a Medicare Advantage plan depends on your healthcare needs and preferences:

Medicare Supplement Plans: These plans work alongside Original Medicare, helping to cover out-of-pocket costs like deductibles and copayments. They provide flexibility in choosing healthcare providers but require separate premiums for the supplement plan and Part B.

Medicare Advantage Plans: These plans are all-in-one alternatives to Original Medicare. They often include prescription drug coverage and may offer additional benefits like dental, vision, and wellness programs. Beneficiaries usually pay a single premium to the private insurer.

The choice between the two depends on factors such as budget, preferred doctors and hospitals, and the desired level of coverage.

9.5. Medicare Cost by Location

Medicare costs can vary by location due to factors such as healthcare provider rates and the availability of Medicare Advantage plans. Premiums, deductibles, and copayments may differ from one region to another. You must consult Medicare resources or insurance providers serving your area to determine your specific costs.

9.6. Conclusion

Medicare is a vital healthcare program for older adults and certain individuals with disabilities. Understanding the different parts of Medicare, enrollment options, and associated costs is essential for making informed decisions about your healthcare coverage. When nearing the age of eligibility, it's advisable to explore your options, consider your healthcare needs, and consult with insurance experts or Medicare counselors to create a plan that best suits your requirements and budget.

Chapter 10
Estate Planning

Understanding estate planning is vital to comprehensive wealth management and legacy planning for investors. Estate planning involves preparing to transfer an individual's assets after their death, ensuring that their wishes are honored, and their loved ones are provided for in the most effective and tax-efficient way possible.

Effective estate planning goes beyond drafting a will. It encompasses a range of considerations and tools, such as trusts, beneficiary designations, powers of attorney, and healthcare directives. Each serves a unique purpose in safeguarding an individual's assets, minimizing estate taxes, and ensuring that decision-making authority is clearly established in case of incapacity.

Key aspects of estate planning include:

Asset Distribution *involves determining who will inherit assets and under what conditions. This can involve specific bequests to individuals, charities, or other organizations.*

Tax Planning*: Understanding and planning for potential estate and inheritance taxes to maximize the value passed on to beneficiaries.*

Healthcare Decisions*: Establish directives for healthcare and appoint someone to make medical decisions if one cannot do so.*

Financial Management*: Choosing a trusted individual or entity to manage financial affairs through a durable power of attorney.*

Guardianship Considerations*: Designating a guardian is critical to estate planning for those with minor children or dependents.*

Trust Formation*: Trusts can be used for various purposes, including asset protection, tax reduction, and specifying terms for asset distribution.*

Investors need to understand that estate planning is not a one-time task but a dynamic process that should be revisited and updated in response to life changes such as marriage, the birth of children, the acquisition of significant assets, or changes in the law.

Without proper estate planning, the distribution of assets can become a lengthy and costly legal process, potentially leading to family disputes and asset value erosion due to taxes and legal fees.

10.1. Introduction to Estate Planning

Estate planning is the process of organizing and arranging one's assets and legal affairs to prepare for the possibility of death or incapacitation. It typically involves creating a will or trust, designating beneficiaries for assets such as life insurance policies and retirement accounts, and making end-of-life decisions such as funeral arrangements. The goal of estate planning is to ensure that one's assets are distributed according to their wishes in the most efficient and tax-advantaged way possible. This can include minimizing probate costs, reducing or eliminating estate taxes, and ensuring that assets are protected from creditors and lawsuits.

Estate planning can also involve creating a plan for the care and management of one's assets in the event of incapacity, such as through a power of attorney or living trust. It is important to consult with a qualified estate planning attorney to help create and implement an estate plan that meets your specific needs and goals.

10.2. Different Types of Trusts

Trusts are versatile estate planning tools that allow individuals to specify how their assets should be managed and distributed. There are various types of trusts, each serving specific purposes:

Revocable Living Trust: A revocable living trust allows the grantor, or person creating the trust, to retain control over the assets placed in the trust during their lifetime. The grantor is also typically the initial trustee and beneficiary of the trust. This means they can change the trust, access the assets in the trust, and receive the income generated by the assets in the trust. Upon the grantor's death, the assets in the trust are distributed to the beneficiaries named in the trust document, according to the terms of the trust. This can help avoid probate and potentially save time and money for the beneficiaries. Additionally, a revocable living trust can be helpful for asset protection and estate tax planning.

Irrevocable Trust: An irrevocable trust is a type of trust that cannot be amended or terminated by the grantor once it has been created. This means that once assets are transferred into the trust, they cannot be taken out or transferred to another party. The grantor also loses control over the assets and cannot use them for their benefit. The purpose of an irrevocable trust is typically to protect assets and reduce the grantor's estate tax liability. A trustee manages the assets in the trust, and its beneficiaries have no control over the assets or how they are managed. The trust document outlines specific instructions on how the assets should be managed and distributed. Some common types of irrevocable trusts include charitable trusts, generation-skipping trusts, and irrevocable life insurance trusts.

Charitable Trust: A charitable trust, with its potential for providing tax benefits to the grantor, is a financially savvy choice. The trust is funded with assets, such as cash, stock, or real estate, which a trustee manages and invests. The income generated by the trust is distributed to the designated charitable organization or cause, providing a tax-efficient way to support a cause.

Special Needs Trust: A special needs trust, also known as a supplemental needs trust, is specifically designed to provide for the financial needs of a person with a disability without affecting their eligibility for government benefits such as Medicaid and Supplemental Security Income (SSI). The trust holds assets for the benefit of the person with a disability, and the trustee is responsible for managing and distributing the assets to pay for the person's supplemental needs, such as medical expenses, education, and other items not covered by government benefits. These trusts can be established by parents, grandparents, or other family members or by the individual with a disability with the help of an attorney. The trust can be funded with cash, property, or other assets and set up to receive ongoing contributions from friends and family. The assets held in the trust are not considered part of the person's estate for Medicaid or SSI eligibility purposes and do not affect their benefits.

Life Insurance Trust: A life insurance trust (LIT) holds and manages life insurance policies. Its purpose is typically to help minimize estate taxes and ensure that the beneficiaries receive the death benefit from the policy tax-efficiently.

An LIT can be either revocable or irrevocable. The grantor can change or dissolve a revocable LIT, while an irrevocable LIT cannot be altered or dissolved once it is set up.

The grantor, also known as the settlor, transfers ownership of a life insurance policy to the trust and names a trustee to manage the policy and distribute the death benefit to the trust's beneficiaries.

The trust then becomes the owner and beneficiary of the life insurance policy, and the death benefit is paid to the trust upon the insured's death rather than to the insured's estate. This can help reduce estate taxes and ensure that the death benefit is distributed according to the grantor's wishes.

It's important to note that the use of life insurance trusts and the benefits they provide may vary depending on the laws of the country or state in which you reside. It's best to consult a qualified estate planning attorney to understand how they may apply to your circumstances.

Family Trust: A family trust is established to benefit a family, typically to preserve family assets, manage family wealth, and provide for family members. Family trusts can be set up as either revocable or irrevocable and can be used for various purposes, such as estate planning, tax planning, and asset protection. The trust assets are managed by a trustee, who is responsible for investing, managing, and distributing the assets according to the terms of the trust. One of the main advantages of a family trust is that it allows the assets to be passed down to future generations without going through probate, which can be costly and time-consuming.

Spendthrift Trust: A spendthrift trust is established to manage and protect a beneficiary's assets deemed financially irresponsible or unable to manage their finances. This type of trust is often set up for beneficiaries who are minors, have a history of financial mismanagement, or have a mental or physical disability. The trustee, appointed by the grantor, can make payments to the beneficiary for their support, education, and maintenance. The trust assets are protected from the beneficiary's creditors, and the beneficiary cannot access the trust assets until a certain age or as determined by the trust document's terms. A spendthrift trust is irrevocable, meaning it cannot be changed or revoked once established.

Totten Trust (Payable-on-Death Account): A Totten trust, also known as a payable-on-death (POD) account, is a type of trust created by a depositor (the grantor) using a bank or brokerage account. The trust is established by adding a POD beneficiary designation to the account. The grantor retains control of the account during their lifetime and can make deposits, withdrawals, and changes to the account as they wish. Upon the grantor's death, the account passes directly to the designated beneficiary, bypassing probate. Totten trusts are typically used for small amounts of money and are relatively easy to set up, but they do not offer the same level of protection and control as more formal types of trusts.

Qualified Personal Residence Trust (QPRT): A Qualified Personal Residence Trust (QPRT) allows the grantor (the person creating the trust) to transfer ownership of their primary residence or vacation home to a trust while retaining the right to live in the property for a specified number of years. At the end of the term, the property is transferred to the trust's beneficiaries. The benefit of a QPRT is that the grantor can transfer the property to the trust at a lower value for gift and estate tax purposes since the grantor retains the right to live in the property for a certain number of years. Additionally, suppose the grantor does not survive the term of the trust. In that case, the property will pass to the beneficiaries outside the grantor's estate and may be eligible for a step-up. It's important to note that a QPRT is a complex estate planning tool and should be set up with the help of a qualified attorney or estate planning professional.

Generation-Skipping Trust (GST): A Generation-Skipping Trust (GST) allows assets to be passed down to the next generation without being subject to estate or gift taxes. This type of trust is typically used to skip a generation of beneficiaries, such as passing assets directly to grandchildren rather than children. An individual establishes the GST, typically including a "skip person" as the beneficiary, such as a grandchild. The assets in the trust are not included in the estate of the grantor or the skip person and, thus, are not subject to estate taxes upon their deaths.

The GST is subject to the Generation-Skipping Transfer (GST) Tax. This tax is imposed on transferring assets to the skip person, but a GST tax exemption can be allocated to gifts or bequests to skip persons. Effective January 1, 2023, the estate and gift tax basic exclusion amount and the generation-skipping transfer (GST) tax exemption are scheduled to increase from $12,060,000 to $12,920,000. GSTs can be helpful in estate planning for high-net-worth individuals or those who wish to provide for future generations tax-efficiently. However, GSTs are complex legal arrangements; consulting with an experienced estate planning attorney is essential before creating one.

NOTE: *Absent legislative action, the basic exclusion amount and GST tax exemption will revert to approximately 50% of their current levels (plus inflation) in 2026.*

10.3. Value of Transfer Upon Death for Accounts

The value of transfer upon death for accounts, also known as the "transfer on death" (TOD) or "payable on death" (POD) designation, refers to the transfer of ownership of an account to a designated beneficiary upon the account holder's death. The TOD or POD designation can be added to various accounts, such as bank accounts, brokerage accounts, and retirement accounts, allowing the account assets to pass directly to the beneficiary without going through probate.

The account holder's death will transfer the account's value to the beneficiary, who can access and use the assets in the account as they see fit. The process for adding a TOD or POD designation to an account varies depending on the type of account and the financial institution. It is important to consult with a financial advisor or attorney to ensure the designation is correctly added.

10.4. Choosing an Estate Planning Attorney

Choosing an estate planning attorney is an important decision, as the attorney will be responsible for helping you create a plan that will protect your assets and provide for your loved ones in the event of your death or incapacity. Some factors to consider when choosing an estate planning attorney include:

Experience: Look for an attorney with experience in estate planning who specializes in the type of planning you need. For example, if you have a complex estate with many assets, you will want to find an attorney with experience handling complex estates.

Credentials: Look for an attorney licensed to practice in your state and a member of professional organizations such as the American Bar Association and the National Academy of Elder Law Attorneys.

Communication: Find an attorney who is easy to communicate with, listens to your concerns and is willing to answer your questions.

Fees: Ask about the attorney's fees and what services are included. Compare fees among attorneys to find one that best fits your budget.

Reputation: Ask other attorneys and professionals in the community for recommendations and look at online reviews.

10.5. Conclusion

Estate planning is an essential aspect of financial planning that ensures your assets are protected and distributed according to your wishes. By understanding the various tools and strategies available, such as trusts and beneficiary designations, and working with a qualified estate planning attorney, you can create a plan that provides for your loved ones, minimizes tax liabilities, and preserves your legacy. Regularly reviewing and updating your estate plan as circumstances change is crucial to ensuring its effectiveness.

Chapter 11
Invest in Yourself

Investing in oneself is arguably the most crucial and impactful investment an individual can make. For investors and professionals alike, dedicating resources to personal development, education, and health can yield significant returns regarding career advancement, financial success, and overall well-being. This concept extends beyond mere financial investments, encompassing time, energy, and effort devoted to self-improvement.

The benefits of self-investment are multifaceted:

Education and Skill Development*: Continuous learning and skill enhancement can lead to better job opportunities, higher earning potential, and staying relevant in a rapidly evolving job market. This might include formal education, online courses, workshops, or certifications.*

Health and Wellness*: Investing in physical and mental health is crucial. Regular exercise, a balanced diet, preventive healthcare, and mental health care improve quality of life, increase productivity, and reduce healthcare costs in the long term.*

Networking and Relationships*: Building and maintaining a professional network can open doors to new opportunities, partnerships, and knowledge sharing. Similarly, nurturing personal relationships is vital for emotional support and overall happiness.*

Financial Literacy*: Understanding personal finance, budgeting, saving, and investing is essential for long-term financial security. Knowledge in these areas empowers individuals to make informed decisions about their finances.*

Personal Branding and Online Presence*: In today's digital world, building a personal brand and maintaining a professional online presence can significantly enhance career opportunities and reputation.*

Work-life Balance and Personal Growth*: Investing time in hobbies, travel, and other personal interests contributes to a well-rounded life.*

This balance is key to creativity, stress reduction, and personal fulfillment.

Investing in oneself requires a proactive and deliberate approach. It's about recognizing that personal growth and well-being are fundamental to success in all other areas of life, including financial investments. By prioritizing self-investment, individuals enhance their lives and are better equipped to contribute positively to their communities and workplaces.

11.1. Introduction to Investing in Yourself

Investing in yourself is allocating time, resources, and effort to enhance personal and professional development. It is a proactive and lifelong self-improvement approach that can increase knowledge, skills, and overall well-being. When you invest in yourself, you're making an investment that can yield substantial returns in various aspects of your life.

11.2. The Importance of Self-Investment

Investing in yourself holds several key benefits:

Skills Development: Acquiring new skills or improving existing ones can enhance your career prospects, increase earning potential, and make you more adaptable to changing job markets.

Personal Growth: Self-investment can lead to personal growth, increased self-awareness, and improved mental and emotional well-being.

Financial Success: Learning about personal finance, budgeting, and investing can help you make informed financial decisions, leading to greater financial stability and wealth accumulation.

Health and Well-Being: Prioritizing self-care, physical fitness, and mental health can lead to a longer, healthier life.

Career Advancement: Professional development and continuous learning can open up new career opportunities and increase your chances of career advancement.

11.3. Ways to Invest in Yourself

There are numerous ways to invest in yourself, including:

Education and Training: Enroll in courses, workshops, or degree programs to acquire new knowledge and skills.

Reading: Regular reading broadens your horizons, keeps you informed, and can improve your critical thinking and communication skills.

Networking: Building and nurturing relationships with peers, mentors, and industry professionals can provide valuable insights and opportunities.

Health and Fitness: Prioritize physical and mental health through regular exercise, proper nutrition, and stress management.

Financial Education: Learn about personal finance, investing, and wealth-building strategies to secure your financial future.

Time Management: Develop time management skills to increase productivity and achieve work-life balance.

Personal Development: Focus on personal growth, self-reflection, and self-awareness to enhance well-being.

11.4. Balancing Self-Investment with Other Priorities

While investing in yourself is essential, balancing other priorities, including family, work, and leisure, is crucial. Effective time management and goal setting can help you allocate time for self-improvement while ensuring you meet other responsibilities.

11.5. Setting SMART Goals

To make the most of your self-investment efforts, set SMART goals:

Specific: Clearly define what you want to achieve.

Measurable: Identify criteria to track your progress.

Achievable: Ensure your goals are realistic and attainable.

Relevant: Align your goals with your values and priorities.

Time-bound: Set a timeline for accomplishing your goals.

11.6. Building a Lifelong Learning Habit

Lifelong learning is a core aspect of self-investment. Cultivate a habit of continuous learning by staying curious, seeking out new experiences, and embracing challenges.

11.7. Conclusion

Investing in yourself is an invaluable commitment that can lead to personal and professional growth, financial success, and improved quality of life. By prioritizing self-improvement, setting goals, and consciously acquiring new knowledge and skills, you can unlock your full potential and enjoy the benefits of a fulfilling and successful life. Remember that self-investment is a lifelong journey that can pay dividends in all aspects of your life.

Chapter 12
Saving for Children's Education

For investors, particularly those with children or planning to start a family, understanding the nuances of saving for children's education is crucial to financial planning. The cost of education, especially higher education, has been steadily rising, making early and strategic planning essential to meet these future expenses without compromising other financial goals.

Several key factors play a role in planning for children's education:

***Early Planning**: Starting early takes advantage of compounding interest and reduces the financial burden as the education date approaches.*

***Understanding Costs**: Being aware of the potential costs of education, including tuition, living expenses, books, and other fees, is vital. These costs vary widely depending on the type of institution (public vs. private, in-state vs. out-of-state) and the level of education (undergraduate, graduate, professional degrees).*

***Savings Vehicles**: Various savings vehicles are designed specifically for education savings. 529 plans and Coverdell Education Savings Accounts are popular in the United States. These accounts offer tax advantages for education savings.*

***Flexible Planning**: It's essential to consider the flexibility of the savings plan. For instance, 529 plans are generally more flexible regarding fund usage and can be transferred among family members.*

***Balancing with Other Financial Goals**: Saving for education should be balanced with other financial objectives, such as retirement savings, emergency funds, and personal investments.*

***Inflation**: Understanding the impact of inflation on future education costs is essential. The value of funds saved might decrease over time, so planning should consider the projected increase in education costs.*

Investors need to approach education savings with a comprehensive understanding of these factors. It is also important to regularly review and adjust the savings plan as family circumstances and education costs evolve. Additionally, many families find it beneficial to involve children in savings efforts, educating them about financial responsibility and the value of education.

Saving for children's education is a significant commitment that requires thoughtful planning and informed decision-making. While it presents challenges, early and strategic planning can ease the financial burden, ensuring children can access educational opportunities without derailing other financial goals.

12.1. Introduction to Saving for Children's Education

Saving for a child's education is a crucial financial goal for many parents and guardians. The cost of higher education has been steadily rising, making it essential to plan and save early to ensure that children have access to quality education without accumulating excessive student loan debt.

12.2. The Importance of Saving for Education

Saving for children's education offers several significant advantages:

Financial Security: By saving in advance, you can help your child avoid the burden of student loans and reduce their financial stress during and after college.

Choice of Schools: Adequate savings allow students to choose the right college or university based on their educational goals rather than financial constraints.

Tax Benefits: Some education savings accounts offer tax advantages, allowing your savings to grow more efficiently.

Teaching Financial Responsibility: Involving your child in savings can help them learn valuable financial skills and responsibilities.

12.3. Types of Education Savings Accounts

There are several types of education savings accounts and plans available to help you save for your child's education:

529 College Savings Plan: State-sponsored plans that offer tax advantages and flexibility in choosing investment options. Funds can be used for qualified higher education expenses.

Coverdell Education Savings Account (ESA): A tax-advantaged account that can be used for both K-12 and higher education expenses, with more flexible investment options.

Custodial Accounts (UGMA/UTMA): Uniform Gift to Minors Act (UGMA) and Uniform Transfers to Minors Act (UTMA) accounts allow you to save for a child's education with potentially favorable tax treatment.

Prepaid Tuition Plans: Some states offer prepaid tuition plans, allowing you to purchase future college credits at today's prices.

12.4. Setting Education Savings Goals

To effectively save for your child's education, you should establish clear goals, considering factors such as the cost of education, the time until your child attends college, and your desired level of financial contribution.

12.5. Creating a Savings Plan

Once you've set education savings goals, create a comprehensive savings plan:

Budgeting: Review your current financial situation and create a budget that allocates a portion of your income to education savings.

Regular Contributions: Consistently contribute to your chosen education savings account, ideally through automatic transfers or payroll deductions.

Asset Allocation: Determine an appropriate investment strategy based on your risk tolerance and the time until your child starts college.

Tax-Efficient Strategies: Maximize tax benefits by understanding and utilizing tax-advantaged accounts and strategies.

12.6. Involving Your Child in the Savings Process

Teaching your child about saving and the cost of education can help instill financial responsibility. Consider involving them in the savings process and discuss the importance of planning for their educational future.

12.7. Financial Aid Considerations

While saving for education is essential, it's also important to understand how savings may impact your child's eligibility for financial aid, including grants and scholarships. Speak with a financial advisor to develop a strategy that maximizes financial aid opportunities.

12.8. Conclusion

Saving for your child's education is a significant financial goal that requires careful planning and dedication. By understanding the available savings options, setting clear goals, and consistently contributing to education savings accounts, you can help ensure your child has the financial resources to pursue their educational dreams. Additionally, involving your child in the process can help them develop valuable financial skills and a sense of responsibility for their education. Early planning and regular contributions are key to achieving your education savings goals.

Chapter 13
College Savings Plans

Understanding college savings plans is a critical element of financial planning for investors with children or plans to support someone's education. As higher education costs continue to rise, these plans offer a structured and tax-advantaged way to save for future educational expenses.

The two primary types of college savings plans in the United States are 529 Plans and Coverdell Education Savings Accounts (ESAs):

529 Plans*: These state-sponsored plans come in two forms — prepaid tuition and education savings. They offer significant tax benefits and high contribution limits, and funds can be used for a range of education-related expenses at accredited institutions. Contributions to a 529 plan are not federally tax-deductible, but earnings grow tax-free, and withdrawals are not taxed for qualified education expenses.*

Coverdell ESAs*: These accounts are similar to 529 plans regarding tax advantages but have lower contribution limits and broader investment options. Coverdell accounts also offer the flexibility to cover primary and secondary education expenses, not just post-secondary education.*

Key aspects of college savings plans include:

Tax Benefits*: Both plans offer tax-free growth and withdrawals for qualified educational expenses.*

Investment Options*: Plans typically offer a range of investment portfolios, including age-based options that automatically become more conservative as the beneficiary approaches college age.*

Contribution Limits*: 529 Plans generally have higher contribution limits, while Coverdell ESAs have lower annual contribution limits.*

Qualified Expenses*: Funds from these accounts can be used for tuition, room and board, fees, books, and other education-related expenses.*

Impact on Financial Aid: Savings in these accounts can impact a student's eligibility for need-based financial aid.

Flexibility and Control: Considerations include who controls the account, the beneficiary designation, and what happens if the beneficiary does not use the funds for education.

Given these plans' long-term nature and specific purposes, investors must carefully consider their options, aligning them with their financial situation and educational goals for their beneficiaries. It's often advisable to consult with a financial advisor to navigate the complexities of these savings vehicles and to stay updated with any changes in legislation that may affect these plans.

13.1. Introduction to College Savings Plans

College savings plans, often 529 plans, are tax-advantaged accounts designed to help individuals and families save for education expenses. These plans are named after Section 529 of the Internal Revenue Code, which provides specific tax benefits for qualified education savings.

13.2. Types of College Savings Plans

There are two primary types of 529 plans:

529 Savings Plans: These plans function like investment accounts, allowing you to contribute money invested in various investment options, such as mutual funds. The goal is for your contributions to grow to cover future education expenses.

529 Prepaid Tuition Plans: These allow you to prepay tuition at eligible colleges or universities at today's prices. Your child or beneficiary receives future tuition benefits at the chosen institution.

13.3. Benefits of College Savings Plans

College savings plans offer several advantages:

Tax Benefits: Earnings in 529 plans grow tax-deferred, and qualified withdrawals are typically tax-free. Some states also offer tax deductions or credits for contributions.

Flexible Beneficiary: You can change the beneficiary of a 529 plan to another eligible family member without penalty.

High Contribution Limits: Many 529 plans have high contribution limits, allowing you to save significant sums for education expenses.

Wide Range of Qualified Expenses: Funds from 529 plans can be used for various qualified education expenses, including tuition, fees, books, and, in some cases, room and board.

13.4. Eligibility and Account Ownership

Generally, anyone can open a 529 plan, and contributors' incomes are not limited. The account owner (often a parent or guardian) controls the account and decides how the funds are used.

13.5. Using 529 Plan Funds

To use funds from a 529 plan, you must follow specific guidelines:

Qualified Expenses: Funds must be used for qualified education expenses at eligible institutions, including colleges, universities, vocational schools, and even some K-12 education expenses.

Non-Qualified Expenses: If you use 529 plan funds for non-qualified expenses, you may incur taxes and penalties on the earnings portion of the withdrawal.

13.6. State-Sponsored 529 Plans

Each U.S. state and the District of Columbia sponsors at least one 529 plan. While many plans are open to residents of any state, some offer additional tax incentives or benefits to residents who invest in their state's plan.

13.7. Comparing 529 Plans

When choosing a 529 plan, consider factors like fees, investment options, and performance. Many resources and online tools are available to help you compare and select the right plan for your needs.

13.8. Contribution Limits and Gifting Strategies

529 plans often have high contribution limits, but there may be gift tax implications if contributions exceed certain thresholds. Strategies like front-loading (making five years' worth of contributions at once) can maximize the benefits of a 529 plan.

13.9. Impact on Financial Aid

529 plan assets may affect a student's eligibility for need-based financial aid. However, the impact is typically lower than other assets, and some states offer protections for 529 plan assets.

13.10. Conclusion

College savings plans, or 529 plans, provide an effective and tax-advantaged way to save for education expenses. Understanding the types of plans available, their benefits, and the rules governing their use can help you make informed decisions about how to best prepare for the cost of education for yourself, your child, or other beneficiaries. Consulting with a financial advisor or education savings specialist can assist you in developing a strategy that aligns with your goals and financial situation.

Chapter 14
Gold Investment

Understanding gold investment is essential for investors as part of a diversified investment strategy. Gold, known for its historic role as a store of value, offers a unique set of characteristics that can make it an attractive asset for many investors.

Investing in gold can serve several purposes:

Diversification*: Gold often has a low correlation with other asset classes like stocks and bonds, making it a useful tool for diversification.*

Hedge against Inflation and Currency Fluctuations*: Gold is traditionally seen as a hedge against inflation and a haven in times of currency devaluation.*

Safe Haven Asset*: Investors often turn to gold as a haven asset in geopolitical or economic uncertainty.*

However, investing in gold also comes with its own set of considerations:

No Income Generation*: Unlike stocks or bonds, gold does not generate income through dividends or interest.*

Storage and Insurance Costs*: Physical gold requires secure storage and insurance, adding to the cost.*

Volatility*: Gold prices can be volatile in the short term.*

Different Forms of Investment:

Physical Gold*: Includes coins, bars, and jewelry.*

Gold Exchange-Traded Funds (ETFs)*: Offers exposure to gold prices without storing physical gold.*

Gold Stocks and Mutual Funds*: Investing in companies that mine, refine, or trade gold.*

Gold Futures and Options*: More complex financial instruments for experienced investors.*

Understanding gold's role in a portfolio is key. It should be considered part of a broader investment strategy, balancing its safety and diversification benefits against its lack of income generation and potential storage costs. The decision to invest in gold and the form in which to do so depends on the individual investor's goals, risk tolerance, and overall investment strategy.

Given gold investment's complexities and unique nature, many investors benefit from professional financial advice to effectively incorporate gold into their portfolios and align with their long-term financial objectives.

14.1. Introduction to Gold Investment

For centuries, gold has been a popular investment and store of value. It is often considered a safe-haven asset and a hedge against economic uncertainty, making it an attractive option for investors looking to diversify their portfolios and protect their wealth.

14.2. The Role of Gold in Investment

Gold serves several important roles in investment portfolios:

Wealth Preservation: Gold is known for preserving wealth over time. It has maintained its value through economic crises and inflation, making it a reliable store of value.

Diversification: Including gold in a diversified portfolio can reduce overall risk because it typically has a low correlation with traditional assets like stocks and bonds. Gold may rise in value when other investments decline, providing a counterbalance.

Inflation Hedge: Gold is often seen as a hedge against inflation. When the purchasing power of fiat currencies erodes due to inflation, the real value of gold tends to rise.

Safe Haven: During economic or geopolitical uncertainty, investors often flock to gold as a safe-haven asset, driving up its price.

14.3. Ways to Invest in Gold

There are several ways to invest in gold:

Physical Gold: You can purchase gold through coins, bars, or jewelry. Storing physical gold may require secure storage options like a bank vault or a home safe.

Gold Exchange-Traded Funds (ETFs): Gold ETFs are investment funds holding physical gold and trading on stock exchanges like regular stocks. They offer a convenient way to invest in gold without owning the physical metal.

Gold Mining Stocks: Investing in gold mining companies exposes you to gold's price movements. However, these stocks can be influenced by factors other than the price of gold, such as operational issues or company-specific risks.

Gold Futures and Options: Sophisticated investors can trade gold futures and options contracts, which derive their value from the price of gold. These instruments are typically used for hedging or speculative purposes.

Gold Certificates: These are certificates issued by banks or financial institutions that represent ownership of a specific quantity of gold. They offer a way to hold gold without the need for physical storage.

14.4. Risks and Considerations

Investing in gold comes with certain risks and considerations:

Price Volatility: The price of gold can be highly volatile, influenced by various factors, including economic data, geopolitical events, and currency fluctuations.

Storage Costs: You may incur secure storage and insurance costs if you own physical gold.

Lack of Income: Gold does not produce income like dividends or interest, making it primarily a capital appreciation asset.

Counterparty Risk: When investing in gold through certificates or ETFs, you have exposure to counterparty risk, meaning you rely on the issuer's ability to deliver the promised gold.

14.5. Taxation of Gold Investments

The tax treatment of gold investments can vary depending on your location and the form of investment. In some jurisdictions, gains from the sale of physical gold may be subject to capital gains tax, while others may offer tax advantages for certain gold investments, such as gold ETFs.

14.6. Conclusion

Gold has long been a favored investment for its role as a store of value, diversification benefits, and potential as a hedge against economic uncertainty. However, it's essential to understand the various ways to invest in gold and the associated risks and costs. Before adding gold to your investment portfolio, consider your investment objectives, risk tolerance, and the overall diversification of your assets. Consulting with a financial advisor or investment professional can help you make informed decisions regarding gold investments.

Chapter 15
Growth Options for Retirement Savings

Understanding growth options for investors planning for retirement is key to ensuring a financially secure and comfortable retirement period. Retirement planning is not just about saving money; it's also about strategically growing those savings over time to outpace inflation and maintain the desired standard of living in retirement.

Investors should consider various growth options, each with different risk-reward profiles:

Stocks and Equities: *Stocks typically offer higher growth potential than other investments, making them suitable for long-term retirement planning. However, they also have higher market volatility.*

Bonds: *Offering more stability than stocks, bonds can provide steady income, making them a common choice for retirees. However, they usually have lower growth potential.*

Mutual Funds and ETFs: *These provide diversification across various assets. Some funds are designed for retirement savings, aligning the risk level with the investor's age and retirement timeline.*

Retirement Accounts: *Accounts like 401(k)s, IRAs (Traditional and Roth), and other pension plans are essential tools. They offer tax advantages that can significantly boost retirement savings growth.*

Real Estate: *Rental properties or investment trusts (REITs) can offer growth potential and income through rent.*

Annuities: *These insurance products can provide guaranteed income in retirement, though they typically offer less growth potential than stocks or mutual funds.*

Alternative Investments: *Includes assets like private equity, commodities, or hedge funds, which can offer diversification and growth but often come with higher risks and fees.*

Understanding these options involves considering factors such as time horizon, risk tolerance, liquidity needs, and the impact of taxes and inflation. As retirement nears, shifting from growth-oriented investments to more income-focused strategies to reduce risk.

Regularly reviewing and adjusting the investment strategy is crucial as personal circumstances and economic conditions change. Many investors also seek advice from financial advisors to tailor their investment approach to their retirement goals and needs. A well-thought-out growth strategy is a cornerstone of successful retirement planning, balancing risk and reward to ensure long-term financial security.

15.1. Introduction to Growth Options

Building a robust retirement nest egg requires not only saving but also investing wisely to achieve long-term growth. Growth options for retirement savings involve strategies and investment vehicles that aim to generate higher returns over time, often focusing on capital appreciation.

15.2. Growth Investment Strategies

Several investment strategies can be employed to promote growth in retirement savings:

Stock Market Investing: Investing in stocks provides the potential for significant long-term growth. Stocks represent ownership in companies and offer the opportunity to benefit from their profitability and growth. While stocks can be volatile, they historically outperform other asset classes over extended periods.

Diversification: Diversifying your investment portfolio across various asset classes, such as stocks, bonds, real estate, and alternative investments, can reduce risk while allowing growth opportunities.

Risk Tolerance: Assess your risk tolerance to determine how much risk you're comfortable taking. Younger investors often have a higher risk tolerance and can allocate a larger portion of their portfolio to growth assets like stocks.

Regular Contributions: Consistently contributing to your retirement accounts, such as 401(k)s and IRAs, allows you to benefit from dollar-cost averaging and compounding over time.

15.3. Investment Goals and Financial Situation

When selecting growth options for retirement savings, consider your investment goals and financial situation:

Time Horizon: The years until your retirement significantly determine your investment strategy. A longer time horizon allows for a more aggressive growth-oriented approach.

Risk Tolerance: Your risk tolerance depends on your comfort with market fluctuations and your ability to endure short-term losses in exchange for the potential for long-term gains.

Income Needs: Consider how much income you'll need in retirement and how your growth investments will contribute to that income.

15.4. Investment Vehicles for Growth

There are several investment vehicles suitable for achieving growth in retirement savings:

401(k) Plans: Employer-sponsored retirement plans often offer a selection of investment options, including stock-based funds, to help employees grow their savings.

Individual Retirement Accounts (IRAs): IRAs provide a tax-advantaged way to invest for retirement, with options for growth investments like stocks and mutual funds.

Mutual Funds: Mutual funds pool money from multiple investors to invest in a diversified portfolio of stocks, bonds, or other securities, making them a convenient way to access growth opportunities.

Exchange-Traded Funds (ETFs): ETFs are similar to mutual funds but trade on stock exchanges. They offer broad market exposure and can be an efficient way to invest in growth-oriented assets.

Stocks: Directly investing in individual stocks allows for greater control over your portfolio. You can select companies you believe have significant growth potential.

Real Estate: Investing in real estate directly or through Real Estate Investment Trusts (REITs) can provide growth and income potential.

Alternative Investments: Some investors explore alternative assets like private equity, hedge funds, and commodities for potential growth opportunities. These investments often come with higher risk and may be less liquid.

15.5. Monitoring and Adjusting

Regularly monitoring your portfolio's performance and re-balancing it as needed is essential to maintaining your chosen level of growth. As you approach retirement, consider gradually shifting your allocation to more conservative assets to protect your gains and reduce risk.

15.6. Conclusion

Growth options for retirement savings are crucial for building a substantial nest egg that can support your desired lifestyle in retirement. By carefully considering your investment goals, risk tolerance, and financial situation, you can choose the right mix of growth-oriented investments and investment vehicles to help you achieve your retirement objectives. Regularly reviewing and adjusting your portfolio is key to ensuring it remains aligned with your long-term growth goals while managing risk effectively. Consulting with a financial advisor or retirement specialist can provide valuable guidance in developing a growth strategy that suits your unique circumstances.

Chapter 16
The Wall Street Approach for Retirees

Understanding the Wall Street approach to investing can be crucial for managing retirement portfolios effectively for retirees or those nearing retirement. This approach, often characterized by strategies employed by financial professionals and institutional investors, can offer insights and methods that may benefit retirees, albeit with particular adaptations to suit their unique needs.

Key considerations for retirees in understanding the Wall Street approach include:

Risk Management*: As retirees typically have a shorter investment horizon and may rely on their investments for income, managing risk becomes a paramount concern. Strategies like diversification, asset allocation, and hedging mitigate volatility and protect capital.*

Income Generation*: Wall Street strategies often include investments that generate regular income, such as dividend-paying stocks, bonds, and other fixed-income securities. This can be crucial for retirees who need a steady income stream.*

Capital Preservation*: While growth is important, preserving capital becomes a priority for retirees. This often involves shifting from aggressive growth strategies to conservative investment options.*

Estate Planning and Wealth Transfer*: Wall Street offers various tools and products for estate planning and wealth transfer, helping retirees ensure their wealth is passed on according to their wishes.*

Tax Efficiency*: Efficient tax planning is vital for retirees to maximize their income and minimize tax liabilities. This includes understanding the tax implications of various investment options and withdrawal strategies.*

Adaptability*: Retirees must adapt Wall Street strategies to suit their risk tolerance, investment time horizon, and income needs. This might mean a more conservative approach than typical Wall Street strategies.*

Professional Advice: Given the complexities of financial markets and the unique challenges of investing during retirement, many retirees benefit from professional financial advice. Financial advisors can tailor Wall Street strategies to individual circumstances, providing guidance on asset allocation, portfolio rebalancing, and tax planning.

In summary, while the Wall Street approach offers sophisticated asset management and growth methods, retirees must carefully adapt these strategies to align with their income generation, capital preservation, and risk tolerance goals. Understanding and selectively integrating Wall Street strategies, often with the help of a financial advisor, can be a valuable part of a retiree's investment strategy.

16.1. Introduction to the Wall Street Approach

The Wall Street approach for retirees refers to an investment strategy that actively manages a retirement portfolio to achieve growth and income while balancing risk. This approach typically involves investing in a mix of stocks, bonds, and other assets to generate returns that can sustain retirement expenses throughout one's retirement years.

16.2. Investment Goals for Retirees

Retirees often have specific investment goals, including:

Capital Preservation: Protecting the principal amount of their retirement savings to ensure they have sufficient funds for the duration of their retirement.

Income Generation: Generating a consistent and reliable stream of income to cover living expenses, medical costs, and other financial needs.

Inflation Protection: Accounting for the impact of inflation, which erodes the purchasing power of money over time.

Estate Planning: Passing on wealth to heirs or charitable organizations while minimizing taxes and administrative hassles.

16.3. Asset Allocation

The Wall Street approach for retirees emphasizes asset allocation as a key strategy:

Stocks: Retirees may maintain a portion of their portfolio in stocks to benefit from potential capital appreciation and dividend income. However, the allocation to stocks typically becomes more conservative as retirees age to manage risk.

Bonds: Bonds are considered a more conservative investment and can provide income and stability to a portfolio. Retirees often allocate some of their assets to bonds to offset stock market volatility.

Cash and Cash Equivalents: Holding cash or cash equivalents (e.g., money market funds) provides liquidity and can serve as a buffer for living expenses and emergencies.

Alternative Investments: Some retirees consider alternative assets like real estate investment trusts (REITs), commodities, or managed futures to diversify their portfolio and potentially enhance returns.

16.4. Income Strategies

Retirees may employ several income strategies within the Wall Street approach:

Dividend Stocks: Investing in stocks of companies with a history of paying dividends can provide a regular income stream.

Bonds: Bonds, especially those with coupon payments, can provide reliable interest income.

Annuities: Some retirees purchase annuities to guarantee a steady income stream for life.

Withdrawal Strategies: Establishing a systematic withdrawal plan, such as the 4% rule, can help retirees manage their portfolio withdrawals to cover living expenses while preserving capital.

16.5. Risk Management

Retirees should focus on risk management to protect their retirement savings:

Diversification: Spreading investments across asset classes and geographic regions can reduce portfolio risk.

Regular Review: Periodically reassess and adjust the portfolio's asset allocation and investment strategy to reflect changing financial goals and market conditions.

Long-Term Perspective: Maintaining a long-term perspective can help retirees weather short-term market fluctuations without making impulsive investment decisions.

16.6. Tax Efficiency

Managing taxes is essential for retirees. Strategies like tax-efficient withdrawal planning and tax-loss harvesting can help optimize tax liabilities in retirement.

16.7. Professional Guidance

Many retirees seek professional financial advisors specializing in retirement planning who can provide personalized guidance based on individual circumstances and goals.

16.8. Conclusion

The Wall Street approach for retirees is a comprehensive investment strategy to provide growth and income during retirement while managing risk. It emphasizes asset allocation, income generation, risk management, and tax efficiency to help retirees achieve their financial objectives. **Retirees should consider their unique goals and risk tolerance when implementing this approach. They may benefit** from working with a qualified financial advisor who can tailor the strategy to their needs and circumstances. By combining prudent investment decisions with careful planning, retirees can strive for financial security and peace of mind during their retirement years.

Chapter 17
Foreign Exchange Investments
Overview

What is Foreign Exchange Investment?

Foreign exchange (forex or FX) investment involves trading currencies in the foreign exchange market. The goal is to profit from changes in the exchange rates between currencies. The forex market is the world's largest and most liquid financial market, with a daily trading volume exceeding $6 trillion.

Basic Concepts

1. **Currency Pairs**: Currencies are traded in pairs (e.g., EUR/USD, GBP/JPY). The first currency in the pair is the base currency, and the second is the quote currency. The exchange rate indicates how much of the quoted currency is needed to buy one unit of the base currency.

2. **Bid and Ask Price**: The bid price is the price at which the market is willing to buy the base currency, and the ask price is the price at which the market is willing to sell it. The difference between these prices is the spread.

3. **Leverage**: Leverage allows traders to control more prominent positions with less capital. For example, a leverage of 100:1 means that for every $1 in your account, you can control $100 in the market. While leverage can amplify profits, it also increases the risk of significant losses.

4. **Pips**: A pip (percentage in point) is a currency pair's most minor price move. For most pairs, a pip is 0.0001. For pairs involving the Japanese yen, a pip is 0.01.

5. **Lots**: Forex is traded in lots. A standard lot is 100,000 units of the base currency, a mini lot is 10,000, and a micro lot is 1,000.

How Forex Trading Works

For a Novice Investor

1. **Learning and Research**: Start with a solid understanding of forex markets. Educational resources, including books, online courses, and webinars, can be very helpful.
2. **Demo Trading**: Use demo accounts brokers provide to practice trading without risking real money. This helps you understand the trading platform and develop strategies.
3. **Choosing a Broker**: Select a reputable forex broker with a user-friendly platform, educational resources, and good customer support. Ensure a recognized authority regulates the broker.
4. **Start Small**: Start with a small investment to limit risk. Use micro or mini lots to get comfortable with trading.
5. **Risk Management**: Implement risk management strategies such as stop-loss orders to limit potential losses. Never invest more than you can afford to lose.
6. **Develop a Trading Plan**: Have a clear trading plan that includes your investment goals, risk tolerance, and strategies for entering and exiting trades.

For an Experienced Investor

1. **Advanced Analysis**: Use technical analysis (charts, indicators) and fundamental analysis (economic data, news events) to make informed trading decisions. Experienced traders often develop their own systems and algorithms.
2. **Diversification**: Diversifying investments across different currency pairs and markets to spread risk. Experienced traders might also trade commodities, stocks, and other financial instruments.

3. **Leverage Management**: Utilize leverage wisely. Experienced traders understand the risks and use leverage to maximize potential gains while managing exposure.
4. **Automated Trading**: Consider using automated trading systems or expert advisors (EAs) to execute trades based on predefined criteria. This can help take advantage of market opportunities 24/7.
5. **Psychological Discipline**: Maintain emotional discipline to stick to the trading plan, avoid overtrading, and manage stress. Experienced traders understand the importance of a clear mind in making objective decisions.
6. **Continuous Learning**: Stay updated with market developments, new trading strategies, and technological advancements. The forex market is dynamic, and continuous learning is crucial for long-term success.

Conclusion Forex trading offers significant opportunities but comes with substantial risks. For novice investors, it's essential to build a strong foundation, start small, and practice risk management. Experienced investors can leverage their knowledge and skills to develop sophisticated strategies and exploit market opportunities. Whether you're a beginner or a seasoned trader, continuous learning and disciplined trading are key to success in the forex market.

Checklists

Checklist of Key Items to Consider When Reviewing a Proposed Annuity

Type of Annuity: Understand if it is a fixed, variable, or indexed annuity.

Payout Options: Consider options like lifetime payouts, period certain, or lump-sum payments.

Surrender Period: Check the length of the surrender period and associated fees.

Fees and Expenses: Identify all costs, including management fees, mortality and expense risk charges, and administrative fees.

Investment Options: For variable annuities, review the available investment choices.

Guaranteed Return: Examine any guaranteed minimum return and under what conditions it applies.

Riders and Additional Features: Understand optional features like death benefits, living benefits, or inflation protection and their associated costs.

Tax Implications: Assess the tax treatment of contributions, growth, and withdrawals.

Financial Strength of the Issuer: Research the financial stability and rating of the insurance company offering the annuity.

Withdrawal Rules and Penalties: Understand the rules and penalties for early withdrawals.

Inflation Protection: Check for an option or rider to protect against inflation.

Portability: See if the annuity can be transferred or rolled over into another retirement account.

Beneficiary Designations: Ensure a clear understanding of how benefits are paid to beneficiaries.

Free Look Period: Confirm if there's a free Look Period to cancel the contract without penalty.

State Guaranty Association Coverage: Check the extent of coverage under your state's guaranty association if the insurer becomes insolvent.

It is important to thoroughly review these factors and consult a financial advisor to ensure the annuity meets your financial goals and needs.

Checklist of Key Items to Review When Purchasing Life Insurance

When purchasing life insurance, it's important to consider various factors to ensure that the policy meets your needs and financial goals. Here's a checklist of key items to review:

Type of Policy: Determine whether you need term life insurance (coverage for a specific period) or permanent life insurance (coverage for life with potential cash value accumulation).

Coverage Amount: Decide how much coverage you need based on factors like income replacement, debts, future education costs for dependents, and funeral expenses.

Premiums: Understand how much you will pay, how often, and whether the premiums are fixed or variable.

Policy Duration: For term life insurance, choose the term length that best matches your needs (e.g., 10, 20, 30 years).

Beneficiary Designation: Carefully select your beneficiaries and understand how to update this information.

Financial Stability of the Insurer: Research the insurance company's financial strength and ability to pay future claims.

Policy Exclusions: Understand what is not covered by the policy, such as deaths due to certain activities or health conditions.

Riders and Additional Benefits: Consider any additional riders or benefits, such as critical illness riders, waiver of premium, or accidental death benefits.

Underwriting Process: Be prepared for the underwriting process, which may include a medical exam and questions about your health, lifestyle, and family medical history.

Guaranteed Renewability: For term policies, check if the policy is renewable without additional medical exams at the end of the term.

Conversion Options: If you have a term policy, understand your options to convert it to a permanent policy without undergoing further medical exams.

Cash Value Component: For permanent policies, understand how the cash value accumulates, how you can access it, and its impact on the death benefit.

Loan Options: If the policy has a cash value, understand the terms for borrowing against it.

Policy Surrender Charges: Be aware of any fees or penalties if you decide to surrender the policy early.

Inflation and Future Needs: Consider whether the coverage amount will be sufficient in the future, accounting for inflation and changes in your financial situation.

Tax Implications: Understand the tax implications of your life insurance policy, both for premiums paid and benefits received.

Review Period: Check for a "free look" period during which you can review and cancel the policy without penalty.

Payment Flexibility: Understand the flexibility in premium payments and any penalties for late payments.

Claim Process: Know the process for filing a claim and the typical time frame for payout.

Professional Advice: If needed, seek advice from a financial advisor or insurance agent to help you choose the right policy and coverage.

This checklist is designed to help you comprehensively review and choose a life insurance policy that best suits your needs and those of your dependents.

Checklist of Key Items to Review When Purchasing an Alternative Investment

When purchasing an alternative investment, which can include assets like private equity, hedge funds, real estate, commodities, and others, it's important to conduct a thorough evaluation. Here's a checklist of key items to review:

Investment Type: Identify the type of alternative investment (e.g., real estate, private equity, hedge funds, collectibles, etc.).

Risk Profile: Understand the specific risks associated with the investment, including market, liquidity, credit, and operational risks.

Return Expectations: Have realistic expectations about potential returns, understanding they may be variable and potentially higher risk.

Investment Horizon: Know the time horizon for the investment, as many alternative investments require longer commitments.

Liquidity Constraints: Assess the liquidity of the investment, as many alternatives have longer lock-up periods and are not easily sold.

Minimum Investment Requirement: Be aware of the minimum investment amount, which can be substantial for many alternative investments.

Fee Structure: Understand all fees involved, including management fees, performance fees, and any other hidden costs.

Tax Implications: Review the potential tax consequences of the investment, as they can vary greatly compared to traditional investments.

Regulatory and Legal Aspects: Ensure compliance with all regulatory and legal requirements related to the investment.

Manager's Track Record: Evaluate the track record and expertise of the investment manager or firm managing the investment.

Diversification Impact: Consider how the investment fits into your overall portfolio and its impact on diversification.

Performance History: Review the investment's historical performance, but be cautious, as past performance does not indicate future results.

Due Diligence on Underlying Assets: Conduct due diligence on the underlying assets or projects within the investment.

Valuation Frequency: Understand how often the investment is valued and the methodology used for valuation.

Redemption Terms: Know the terms for redeeming your investment, including notice periods and any penalties.

Reporting and Transparency: Look for investments with transparent and frequent reporting to keep investors informed.

Investor Eligibility: Ensure you meet the eligibility criteria for investing, which may include being an accredited or qualified investor.

Investment Thesis and Strategy: Understand the investment strategy and how it aligns with your objectives and market views.

Economic and Market Conditions: Consider current forecasted economic and market conditions and how they might impact the investment.

Professional Advice: Seek advice from a financial advisor or investment professional, especially if you are new to alternative investments.

This checklist covers essential considerations for evaluating an alternative investment, helping to make an informed decision that aligns with your financial goals and risk tolerance.

Checklist of Key Items to Review When Seeking Professional Investment Advice

When seeking professional investment advice, conducting a thorough review is crucial to ensure you are working with the right advisor and that their guidance aligns with your financial goals. Here is a checklist of key items to review:

Credentials and Qualifications: Check the advisor's credentials (e.g., CFP, CFA, CPA) to ensure they are qualified to provide financial advice.

Registration and Licensing: Verify that the advisor is registered with the relevant regulatory bodies (like the SEC or FINRA in the U.S.).

Experience: Consider the advisor's expertise in the industry, specifically in areas relevant to your financial needs.

Specialization: Determine if the advisor specializes in certain areas, such as retirement planning, estate planning, or wealth management.

Reputation and References: Research their reputation and ask for references from current or past clients.

Investment Philosophy: Understand the advisor's investment philosophy to ensure it aligns with your investment style and risk tolerance.

Services Offered: Review the services offered (e.g., investment management, financial planning, tax advice) and ensure they meet your needs.

Fee Structure: Understand how the advisor is compensated (e.g., fee-only, commission-based, fee-based) and ensure transparency of all fees.

Conflict of Interest: Inquire about any potential conflicts of interest the advisor may have.

Communication and Accessibility: Discuss how often the advisor will communicate with you and their availability for meetings or consultations.

Performance Reporting: Check how the advisor will report investment performance and how often.

Client Profile: Ensure the advisor typically works with clients with similar profiles to yours (regarding assets, financial goals, and life stage).

Portfolio Customization: Find out if the advisor offers personalized investment strategies or uses a one-size-fits-all approach.

Ongoing Education and Training: Check if the advisor stays updated with current market trends, laws, and strategies through ongoing education.

Dispute Resolution Process: Understand the process for handling any disputes or disagreements that may arise.

Risk Management Strategies: Ask about the strategies used for risk assessment and management.

Data Security and Privacy: Ensure that your personal and financial information will be kept secure and confidential.

Termination Policy: Know the terms for ending the relationship, including any fees or notice periods.

Alignment with Financial Goals: Ensure the advisor understands and aligns with your short-term and long-term financial goals.

Trust and Comfort Level: Finally, assess your level of trust and comfort with the advisor, as a strong, trusting relationship is key.

This checklist will help you evaluate potential investment advisors, ensuring you find a professional who is well-qualified, transparent, and aligned with your financial objectives.

Checklist of Key Items to Review When Considering Investment Options

When considering investment options, conducting a comprehensive review is essential to ensure that your choices align with your financial goals, risk tolerance, and investment horizon. Here is a checklist of key items to review:

Investment Goals: Define your short-term and long-term financial objectives. This will guide your investment strategy and choice of assets.

Risk Tolerance: Assess your willingness and ability to bear risk. This will help you select investments that match your comfort level with volatility.

Investment Horizon: Determine your time frame for investing. Short-term goals may require more liquid and less volatile investments, while long-term goals might allow for higher-risk, higher-return options.

Asset Allocation: Consider how the investment fits into your overall asset allocation, balancing stocks, bonds, real estate, commodities, etc., to diversify risk.

Liquidity Needs: Evaluate how quickly and easily you can convert the investment into cash. Some investments, like real estate or certain funds, may have lower liquidity.

Costs and Fees: Understand all associated costs, including management fees, transaction fees, and any other charges that can affect returns.

Tax Implications: Consider the investment's tax consequences, including tax rates on dividends, interest income, and capital gains.

Historical Performance: Review past performance, remembering that past results do not guarantee future returns.

Market Conditions: Analyze current market trends and economic indicators that could impact the performance of your investments.

Investment Research: Conduct thorough research or consult research reports on specific investments to understand their potential risks and returns.

Regulatory and Compliance Issues: Ensure that the investment and the entity offering it comply with relevant regulations.

Performance Benchmarks: Compare the investment's performance against appropriate benchmarks to assess its relative performance.

Investment Manager's Track Record: If the investment is managed, evaluate the manager's or management team's track record and expertise.

Volatility and Performance Metrics: Understand key metrics like standard deviation, beta, and Sharpe ratio to assess risk and return characteristics.

Investment Thesis: Be clear about why a particular investment is expected to succeed and how it fits into broader market dynamics.

Diversification Benefits: Assess how the investment contributes to the diversification of your overall portfolio.

Exit Strategy: Clearly understand how and when you might liquidate the investment.

Investor Reviews and Reputation: Look at reviews and the reputation of the investment firm or product.

Inflation Considerations: Consider the potential impact of inflation on your investment returns.

Professional Advice: If needed, consult a financial advisor for personalized advice tailored to your situation.

This checklist helps you make informed decisions and choose investments that are well-suited to your personal financial situation and goals.

Checklist of Key Items to Consider When Purchasing a Bond

When purchasing a bond, conducting a thorough review is crucial to ensure that the investment aligns with your financial goals and risk tolerance. Here's a checklist of key items to review when purchasing a bond:

Type of Bond: Understand whether it's a government bond (like a Treasury or municipal bond) or a corporate bond, as the risk and return profiles differ.

Credit Rating: Check the bond's credit rating, which indicates the issuer's creditworthiness and the risk of default.

Interest Rate: Review the bond's interest rate (coupon rate) to determine the income you'll receive.

Yield to Maturity (YTM): Calculate or review the YTM, which reflects the total return anticipated on the bond if it is held until it matures.

Maturity Date: Know when the bond will mature, and the principal will be repaid. Consider how this aligns with your investment horizon.

Price: Determine if the bond is being sold at par, a discount, or a premium, and understand how this affects your return.

Call Features: If applicable, understand any call features that allow the issuer to redeem the bond early.

Market Conditions: Consider the current interest rate environment and economic conditions, as they can affect bond prices and yields.

Inflation Risk: Evaluate the potential impact of inflation on the bond's return, especially for long-term bonds.

Liquidity: Assess the bond's liquidity or how easily you can sell it before maturity without significantly affecting its price.

Tax Implications: Understand any tax considerations, especially for municipal bonds, which might offer tax advantages.

Diversification: If you're buying individual bonds, consider how they fit into your overall investment portfolio in terms of diversification.

This checklist covers essential factors for evaluating a bond investment, helping you make an informed decision.

Checklist of Key Items to Review When Considering a CD Investment

When considering a Certificate of Deposit (CD) investment, it's important to carefully evaluate various aspects to ensure that it aligns with your financial goals and circumstances. Here is a checklist of key items to review:

Interest Rate: Check the annual percentage yield (APY) to understand how much interest you will earn.

Term Length: Determine the duration of the CD. Common terms range from a few months to several years.

Minimum Deposit Requirement: Know the minimum amount required to open the CD.

Early Withdrawal Penalties: Understand the penalties for withdrawing your money before the CD matures, as they can significantly reduce your earnings.

Renewal Policies: Be aware of the automatic renewal policy (if any) and the grace period during which you can withdraw funds without penalty after maturity.

Institution's Credibility: Ensure the financial institution is reputable and insured by the FDIC (Federal Deposit Insurance Corporation) or a similar entity.

Interest Compounding Frequency: Find out how often interest is compounded, as more frequent compounding can lead to higher returns.

Liquidity Needs: Consider your need for liquidity. A CD might not be the best choice if you need access to your funds before the CD matures.

Rate Comparison: Compare rates from different institutions to find the best deal. Online banks often offer higher rates than traditional banks.

Inflation Risk: Consider the potential impact of inflation on your investment, especially for longer-term CDs.

Tax Implications: Understand the tax treatment of the interest you earn and how it affects your overall tax situation.

Callable CDs: If considering a callable CD, understand the terms and the potential for the bank to close the CD early.

Laddering Strategy: Consider a CD laddering strategy, in which you invest in CDs with different maturity dates to balance higher rates and access to funds.

Fees and Charges: Check for any additional fees or charges associated with the CD.

Investment Diversification: Assess how the CD investment fits into your portfolio and diversification strategy.

Interest Payment Options: Understand the options for receiving interest payments, whether reinvested, paid out to another account, or paid at maturity.

Market Conditions: Consider the current and expected future interest rate environment, as it can impact the attractiveness of CD rates.

Special Features: Some CDs offer special features like bump-up rates or add-on deposits. Understand these features and whether they benefit your investment strategy.

Financial Goals Alignment: Ensure the CD aligns with your financial goals, risk tolerance, and time horizon.

Professional Advice: If unsure, consult with a financial advisor to determine if a CD is a suitable investment for your specific needs.

By carefully reviewing these items, you can make a more informed decision about whether a CD investment is right for your financial situation.

Checklist of Key Items to Review When Considering a Real Estate Investment

When considering a real estate investment, it's essential to thoroughly evaluate various aspects to ensure that the investment aligns with your financial goals and risk tolerance. Here is a checklist of key items to review:

Property Type: Determine whether you're investing in residential, commercial, industrial, or retail property. Each type has different market dynamics and risks.

Location: Evaluate the location for potential growth, demand, accessibility, and neighborhood stability. Location is a critical factor in real estate valuation.

Market Analysis: Conduct a thorough market analysis to understand current trends, property values, rental rates, and the area's economic health.

Property Condition: Assess the physical condition of the property, including age, structural integrity, and need for repairs or renovations.

Legal and Zoning Issues: Check for any legal issues, property disputes, or zoning restrictions that could affect the property's use or value.

Return on Investment (ROI): Calculate the potential ROI, considering rental income, property appreciation, and tax benefits.

Financing Options: Understand your financing options, interest rates, loan terms, and your ability to qualify for a mortgage.

Cash Flow Analysis: Conduct a cash flow analysis to assess the property's income potential versus ongoing expenses like mortgage payments, property taxes, insurance, and maintenance.

Tax Implications: Consider the tax implications, including property taxes, deductions for mortgage interest, and potential capital gains tax.

Rental Market: If the property is for rental, evaluate the local rental market, including demand, typical rent, and tenant quality.

Insurance Requirements: Determine the type and cost of insurance needed to protect your investment.

Property Management: Decide if you will manage the property yourself or hire a company.

Exit Strategy: Have a clear exit strategy, whether it's selling the property or holding it long-term for passive income.

Resale Value: Consider the potential resale value and factors influencing future property values.

Environmental Assessments: Check for any environmental issues or hazards on the property or in the area.

Long-Term Market Potential: Evaluate the property's and the area's long-term prospects, considering future development plans and economic forecasts.

Liquidity Considerations: Realize that real estate is not a liquid asset, and selling can be time-consuming.

Ownership Structure: Decide on the best ownership structure for your situation, considering aspects like liability and tax efficiency.

Diversification: Assess how the investment fits into your overall investment portfolio in terms of diversification.

Professional Advice: For expert guidance, consult real estate professionals such as agents, lawyers, and financial advisors.

By methodically reviewing these items, you can make a more informed decision about whether real estate investment is suitable for your financial situation and goals.

Checklist of Key Items to Review When Considering Taking Social Security

When considering taking Social Security benefits, several key factors must be evaluated to make an informed decision that aligns with your financial planning and retirement goals. Here's a checklist of key items to review:

Full Retirement Age (FRA): Know your FRA, as it affects your monthly benefit amount. Claiming before FRA reduces your benefit, while delaying increases it.

Benefit Amount at Different Ages: Understand how your monthly benefit changes based on the age at which you start taking Social Security. Benefits increase for each year you delay up to age 70.

Life Expectancy: When estimating your life expectancy, consider your health and family history, as this impacts the total benefits you might receive over time.

Employment Status: If you're working and haven't reached FRA, understand how your earnings might temporarily reduce your benefits.

Spousal Benefits: Review eligibility and strategies for spousal benefits, especially if one spouse has a significantly lower lifetime earnings record.

Survivor Benefits: Understand how your decision impacts survivor benefits for your spouse if you pass away.

Other Retirement Income: Consider your other sources of retirement income and how Social Security fits into your overall retirement plan.

Break-Even Analysis: Perform a break-even analysis to understand the long-term financial impact of taking benefits at different ages.

Inflation and Cost-of-Living Adjustments (COLAs): Social Security benefits are adjusted for inflation, so factor this into your planning.

Taxes on Benefits: Understand how your benefits may be taxed based on your retirement income.

Medicare Enrollment: You must enroll in Medicare at age 65, regardless of whether you're receiving Social Security benefits.

Impact of Divorce: Review the rules for claiming benefits based on your ex-spouse's work record if you are divorced.

Other Government Pensions: If you receive a pension from a job not covered by Social Security, it might affect your Social Security benefits.

Financial Needs: Assess your current financial needs and how they might be met by starting Social Security benefits at different ages.

Long-Term Financial Security: Weigh the decision regarding your long-term financial security and retirement planning.

Investment Strategy: Consider how taking Social Security early or late integrates with your overall investment strategy.

Health Insurance Costs: Understand how taking Social Security early might affect your health insurance costs, especially if you're not yet eligible for Medicare.

Future Policy Changes: Stay informed about potential Social Security program changes that might affect your benefits.

Professional Advice: Consult with a financial advisor to understand how your Social Security decision impacts your financial plan.

Personal Preferences and Lifestyle: Finally, consider your personal preferences, lifestyle choices, and retirement goals in making your decision.

This checklist can help guide your decision-making when considering when to start taking Social Security benefits.

Checklist of Key Items to Review When Considering a 401(k) or an IRA

When considering whether to invest in a 401(k) or an Individual Retirement Account (IRA), evaluating various factors to make an informed decision that aligns with your retirement goals and financial situation is important. Here's a checklist of key items to review:

Eligibility Requirements: Check the eligibility criteria for both a 401(k) and an IRA, as they have different rules regarding income, employment status, and contribution limits.

Contribution Limits: Understand the annual contribution limits for each option. Typically, 401(k)s have higher contribution limits than IRAs.

Employer Match: If your employer offers a 401(k) with a matching contribution, factor in this significant benefit as it's essentially free money.

Investment Options: Compare the investment options available in each plan. 401(k)s often have a limited selection, while IRAs typically offer a wider range of investment choices.

Fees and Expenses: Be aware of the costs and expenses associated with each account type, as high fees can erode investment returns over time.

Tax Treatment: Understand the different tax treatments. Traditional 401(k)s and IRAs offer tax-deferred growth, while Roth options provide tax-free growth.

Withdrawal Rules and Penalties: Familiarize yourself with the withdrawal rules, including the age for required minimum distributions (RMDs) and penalties for early withdrawal.

Loan Options: 401(k) plans may offer loan options, whereas IRAs do not.

Rollover Considerations: If you have an existing 401(k) from a previous employer, consider the pros and cons of rolling it over into an IRA.

Income Tax Considerations: When deciding between a traditional and Roth option, consider your current and expected future tax bracket.

Financial Goals: Align your choice with your long-term financial goals, including your retirement timeline and income needs.

Risk Tolerance: Select a plan that matches your risk tolerance and investment style.

Portability: Understand the portability of each account. An IRA remains with you regardless of your employment status, while a 401(k) is tied to your current employer.

Estate Planning: Consider how each account type fits into your estate planning, especially regarding beneficiary designations and inheritance rules.

Catch-Up Contributions: If you are age 50 or older, check the catch-up contribution limits for each option.

Convenience and Administration: Consider the ease of managing each account type, including online access, customer service, and administrative support.

Diversification: Ensure that your choice allows for adequate diversification of your retirement savings.

Protection from Creditors: Be aware of each option's level of protection from creditors, as 401(k)s often have stronger legal protections.

Inflation Considerations: Consider how each option helps you manage the impact of inflation on your retirement savings.

Professional Advice: Consult with a financial advisor to understand how a 401(k) or an IRA fits into your overall financial plan and to get personalized advice based on your situation.

By carefully reviewing these items, you can make a more informed decision about which retirement savings option is best for you.

Checklist of Key Items to Review When Considering Taking Medicare

When considering enrolling in Medicare, it's crucial to understand the various parts, options, and implications to make an informed decision that aligns with your healthcare needs and financial situation. Here's a checklist of key items to review:

Eligibility and Enrollment Periods: Understand when you are eligible for Medicare (usually at age 65) and the specific enrollment periods to avoid late enrollment penalties.

Understanding Different Parts of Medicare: Familiarize yourself with the different parts:

>**Part A (Hospital Insurance)**: Covers inpatient hospital stays, care in a skilled nursing facility, hospice care, and home health care.

>**Part B (Medical Insurance)**: Covers certain doctors' services, outpatient care, medical supplies, and preventive services.

>**Part C (Medicare Advantage Plans)**: A type of Medicare health plan offered by private companies that contract with Medicare.

>**Part D (Prescription Drug Coverage)**: Adds prescription drug coverage to Original Medicare.

Medicare Advantage vs. Original Medicare: Compare the benefits of Original Medicare (Parts A and B) with Medicare Advantage Plans (Part C), considering factors like coverage, costs, provider networks, and geographic availability.

Prescription Drug Needs: If choosing Original Medicare, consider whether you need a separate Part D plan for prescription drugs.

Supplemental Coverage (Medigap): If you opt for Original Medicare, evaluate whether you need a Medigap policy to cover gaps in Parts A and B, such as deductibles and co-payments.

Costs: Understand the costs associated with each part of Medicare, including premiums, deductibles, co-pays, and coinsurance.

Provider Networks: Check if the plan you are considering covers your preferred healthcare providers and hospitals.

Coverage Limitations and Exclusions: Understand what is not covered by Medicare, such as long-term care, routine dental and vision care, hearing aids, or acupuncture.

Travel Coverage: If you travel frequently, check how each plan covers you outside your home state or abroad.

Income-Related Monthly Adjustment Amount (IRMAA): Be aware that high-income individuals may pay higher premiums for Part B and Part D.

Review Annual Changes: Medicare plans can change annually. Review your coverage each year during the open enrollment period to ensure it meets your needs.

Coordination with Other Insurance: Understand how Medicare works with your existing insurance, such as employer-sponsored coverage or veterans' benefits.

Late Enrollment Penalties: Be aware of late enrollment penalties for Part B and Part D, which can increase your premiums.

Appeals and Grievances: If you disagree with a coverage or payment decision, know the process for filing appeals or grievances.

Preventive Services and Wellness Programs: Take advantage of preventive services and wellness programs that may be offered at no additional cost.

Financial Assistance Programs: If you have limited income and resources, check if you qualify for programs like Medicaid, Medicare Savings Programs, or Extra Help for prescription drugs.

Healthcare Needs Assessment: Assess your current and anticipated healthcare needs, including chronic conditions or treatments.

Information and Counseling Services: Use available resources, like the State Health Insurance Assistance Program (SHIP), for free, personalized counseling about Medicare.

Long-Term Planning: Consider how your choice fits into your long-term health planning and financial situation.

Professional Advice: Consult a healthcare advisor or insurance specialist for personalized advice.

Checklist of Key Items to Review When Considering Estate Planning

Estate planning must ensure your assets are distributed according to your wishes and minimize the burden on your loved ones. Here's a checklist of key items to review when considering estate planning:

Inventory of Assets: Compile a comprehensive list of your assets, including real estate, bank accounts, investments, retirement accounts, insurance policies, and personal property.

Family Dynamics: Consider the dynamics of your family and how they might affect the distribution of your estate.

Will Preparation: Ensure you have a legally valid will that clearly outlines how you want your assets to be distributed.

Trusts: Decide if setting up a trust is beneficial for managing your estate, protecting assets, minimizing taxes, or caring for a family member.

Beneficiary Designations: Review and update beneficiary designations on retirement accounts, life insurance policies, and other assets.

Guardianship Decisions: If you have minor children, choose a guardian and arrange their care and financial support.

Healthcare Directives: Establish healthcare directives, including a living will and healthcare power of attorney, to outline your wishes for medical treatment if you become incapacitated.

Durable Power of Attorney: Appoint someone to manage your affairs if you cannot.

Life Insurance: Assess your coverage to ensure it meets your family's needs, especially if you have dependents.

Debt and Taxes: Understand your liabilities, including debts and potential estate taxes, and how they will be handled.

Charitable Giving: Consider any charitable contributions you wish to make through your estate.

Business Succession Planning: If you own a business, develop a plan for transferring or selling it.

Estate Liquidity: Ensure there is enough liquidity in your estate to cover debts, taxes, and other expenses without the forced sale of assets.

Funeral Arrangements: Outline your wishes for funeral arrangements and consider setting aside funds for these expenses.

Estate Executor: Choose an executor or personal representative who will manage the distribution of your estate.

Legal and Financial Advice: Consult with estate planning attorneys, financial advisors, and tax professionals to ensure your plan is comprehensive and complies with current laws.

Document Storage: Safely store your estate planning documents and let your executor and family members know where to find them.

Review and Update Regularly: Review and update your estate plan regularly, especially after major life events like marriage, divorce, the birth of a child, or significant changes in assets.

Digital Assets: Include plans for your digital assets, such as social media accounts, digital currencies, and online accounts.

Communicating with Family: Consider discussing your estate plans with your family to prepare them and potentially prevent conflicts.

By methodically reviewing these items, you can create a comprehensive estate plan that safeguards your assets, honors your wishes, and provides for your loved ones.

Checklist of Key Items to Review When Considering Saving for Children's Education

Saving for your children's education is an important financial goal for many parents. Here's a checklist of key items to review when considering saving for your children's education:

Start Early: Save as early as possible to take advantage of compound interest and reduce the financial burden later.

Estimate the Costs: Research the potential education costs, including tuition, books, supplies, accommodation, and living expenses. Consider the possibility of future cost increases due to inflation.

Set a Savings Goal: Establish a clear savings goal based on the estimated costs and the years until your child starts their education.

Choose the Right Savings Vehicle: Consider various savings options, such as 529 plans, Coverdell Education Savings Accounts, custodial accounts (UGMA/UTMA), or regular savings accounts. Each has different tax implications, contribution limits, and flexibility in terms of use.

Understand Tax Benefits: Be aware of the tax advantages associated with different education savings accounts, such as tax-free growth or deductions on contributions.

Regular Contributions: To stay consistent, set up regular contributions to the education fund, possibly through automatic transfers.

Investment Strategy: If you use investment accounts, decide on an investment strategy that aligns with your risk tolerance and the time horizon until the funds are needed.

Review and Adjust Over Time: Periodically review and adjust your savings plan and investment choices, especially as your child approaches college age.

Explore Scholarships and Grants: Research scholarships, grants, and other financial aid that can reduce the amount you need to save.

Involve Family Members: Consider involving grandparents or other family members who may wish to contribute to your child's education fund.

Balance with Other Financial Goals: Ensure education savings are balanced with other financial priorities, including retirement and emergency funds.

Understand Withdrawal Rules: Be clear on the rules and penalties for withdrawing funds from education savings accounts, especially if the money is not used for qualified education expenses.

Consider Student Loans: Understand student loans' role in financing your child's education and the implications of potential debt.

Education on Personal Finance: Teach your child about personal finance, saving, and the value of education to foster a responsible attitude toward money and investment in their future.

Flexibility for Changing Plans: Recognize that your child's educational aspirations may change over time and choose savings options that offer some flexibility.

Cost Reduction Strategies: Consider cost reduction strategies such as attending community college first, applying for in-state tuition, or choosing a less expensive institution.

Financial Aid Impact: Understand how your savings might affect financial aid eligibility.

Professional Advice: Consult a financial advisor for personalized advice tailored to your situation and goals.

Alternative Education Paths: Be open to alternative education paths, such as vocational training, online courses, or gap years, which might influence your saving strategy.

Insurance Considerations: Ensure you have adequate insurance to protect your family's financial stability, which will indirectly support your education savings goals.

By methodically reviewing these items, you can create a well-rounded plan to save for your children's education and support their academic goals.

Checklist of Key Items to Review When Considering College Savings Plans

When considering college savings plans, reviewing various aspects is important to ensure you choose a plan that aligns with your financial goals and educational needs. Here's a checklist of key items to review:

Types of College Savings Plans: Understand the different college savings plans available, such as 529 plans, Coverdell Education Savings Accounts (ESAs), custodial accounts (UGMA/UTMA), and savings bonds.

529 Plan Options: If you are considering a 529 plan, differentiate between prepaid tuition plans and education savings plans: research state-specific plans and their benefits.

Tax Advantages: Review each savings plan's tax benefits, including federal and state tax deductions or credits, tax-deferred growth, and tax-free withdrawals for qualified education expenses.

Contribution Limits: Understand the contribution limits for each type of savings plan, as they can vary significantly.

Investment Options: Evaluate the investment options available in each plan, including the types of funds offered and the ability to change investment choices.

Control of Funds: Determine who will control the funds (parent or child) and how this impacts the plan, particularly for UGMA/UTMA custodial accounts.

Impact on Financial Aid: Understand how each type of college savings plan affects eligibility for need-based financial aid.

Qualified Expenses: Learn what expenses are considered qualified under each plan, such as tuition, room and board, textbooks, and other educational expenses.

Flexibility in Use of Funds: Check the flexibility in using the funds, including transferring funds to another beneficiary or using them for non-traditional education paths.

Plan Fees and Expenses: Be aware of any fees or expenses associated with the college savings plan, such as enrollment fees, annual maintenance fees, and investment management fees.

Withdrawal Rules and Penalties: Understand the rules and potential penalties for non-qualified withdrawals, including the tax implications.

State-Specific Benefits: If considering a state-sponsored 529 plan, evaluate any additional state-specific benefits, such as state income tax breaks.

Performance Tracking: Consider how you will track the performance of your investments within the savings plan and the process for making changes if necessary.

Gift and Estate Tax Benefits: For 529 plans, review the gift and estate tax benefits, including the option for accelerated gifting.

Plan Sponsor and Reputation: Research the plan sponsor's reputation and the historical performance of the plan.

Inflation Considerations: Factor in the potential impact of inflation on education costs and whether your savings plan can keep pace.

Regular Contributions: Set up a plan for regular contributions to the college savings plan to maximize growth potential.

Changing Educational Landscape: Stay informed about changes in the educational landscape, such as tuition trends and the evolving value of different types of degrees.

Professional Advice: Consult a financial advisor specializing in education planning to get personalized advice.

Review and Adjust Plan: Regularly review and, if necessary, adjust your college savings plan to align with changing educational goals and financial circumstances.

By thoroughly reviewing these items, you can decide on the best way to save for college and support your or your child's educational future.

Checklist of Key Items to Review When Considering Gold Investment

Investing in gold can be a strategic move for diversification and hedging against inflation and economic uncertainties. Here's a checklist of key items to review when considering an investment in gold:

Investment Objectives: Clarify why you are considering gold as an investment — whether for diversification, as a hedge against inflation, or for other reasons.

Forms of Gold Investment: Understand the different ways to invest in gold, including physical gold (bullion, coins), gold ETFs (Exchange Traded Funds), gold mutual funds, gold mining stocks, and gold futures and options.

Purity and Authenticity: Verify the purity, authenticity, and quality of physical gold. Look for hallmarks and certifications.

Storage and Security: Consider safe storage options for physical gold, such as a safe deposit box or a secure home safe. Assess the associated costs and risks.

Market Conditions: Analyze current market conditions, including gold prices and economic indicators that impact gold prices, like inflation rates, currency values, and interest rates.

Historical Performance: Review the historical performance of gold as an investment, recognizing that past performance does not guarantee future results.

Liquidity: Understand the liquidity of your gold investment. Physical gold may be less liquid than gold ETFs or stocks.

Transaction Costs: Be aware of transaction costs, including commissions, buying premiums, selling discounts, and management fees for ETFs or mutual funds.

Tax Implications: Familiarize yourself with the tax considerations of investing in gold, particularly capital gains tax.

Risk Assessment: Assess the risks associated with gold investments, including price volatility and potential loss of value.

Diversification: Consider how gold fits into your overall investment portfolio in terms of diversification and risk management.

Time Horizon: Determine your investment horizon, as gold may be more suitable for long-term holding.

Regulatory and Legal Considerations: Be aware of any legal and regulatory considerations, especially if investing in gold derivatives or international markets.

Economic and Geopolitical Factors: Understand how global economic and geopolitical factors can influence gold prices.

Gold Mining Companies: Before investing in gold mining stocks, research the companies' financial health, production levels, and growth potential.

Impact of Currency Fluctuations: Consider how currency fluctuations affect gold prices, especially if you invest in an international gold market.

Investment Reviews and Analysis: Consult investment reviews and analysis from credible sources to make informed decisions.

Inflation Protection: Evaluate gold's role as an inflation hedge in your portfolio.

Investment Size: Decide on the size of your investment in gold relative to your overall investment portfolio.

Professional Advice: If you are new to gold investing, consider seeking advice from financial advisors or investment experts.

By thoroughly reviewing these items, you can make a more informed decision about whether investing in gold aligns with your financial goals and risk tolerance.

Checklist of Key Items to Review When Considering Growth Options for Retirement Savings

When considering growth options for retirement savings, it's crucial to evaluate various aspects to ensure that your strategy aligns with your retirement goals, risk tolerance, and time horizon. Here's a checklist of key items to review:

Retirement Goals: Define your retirement goals, including the age at which you plan to retire and the lifestyle you envision during retirement.

Current Financial Status: Assess your financial situation, including your total savings, debts, and regular income.

Risk Tolerance: Determine your risk tolerance level to guide your investment decisions.

Investment Mix (Asset Allocation): Decide on an appropriate mix of stocks, bonds, and other assets to balance growth potential with risk.

Diversification: To mitigate risk, ensure your portfolio is diversified across different asset classes, sectors, and geographies.

Retirement Accounts: Maximize contributions to retirement accounts like 401(k)s, IRAs, or Roth IRAs, considering their tax advantages and contribution limits.

Tax Efficiency: Understand the tax implications of your investments and plan for tax-efficient growth and withdrawal strategies.

Review Existing Investments: Regularly review and adjust your existing investments to ensure they align with your changing risk tolerance and retirement timeline.

Inflation Consideration: Factor in inflation when planning for retirement savings growth to maintain your purchasing power.

Social Security Benefits: Estimate your potential Social Security benefits and factor them into your overall retirement plan.

Healthcare Costs: Consider future healthcare costs, including long-term care, and how they will impact your retirement savings.

Emergency Fund: Maintain an emergency fund to avoid dipping into retirement savings for unexpected expenses.

Debt Management: Work towards reducing high-interest debt, which can hinder the growth of your retirement savings.

Automatic Savings Plan: Set up automatic transfers to your retirement accounts to consistently build your savings.

Professional Financial Advice: Consider seeking advice from a financial planner or advisor to develop a personalized retirement savings strategy.

Investment Costs: Be aware of the costs associated with different investment options, including management fees and expense ratios.

Retirement Income Streams: Explore various options for creating steady income streams during retirement, such as annuities or dividend-paying stocks.

Estate Planning: Incorporate estate planning into your retirement strategy to ensure your assets are distributed according to your wishes.

Withdrawal Strategy: Plan a withdrawal strategy for retirement to ensure that your savings last and minimize tax liabilities.

Continued Learning and Adaptation: Stay informed about financial markets, new investment options, and changes in tax laws that could affect your retirement savings.

By carefully reviewing these items, you can develop a comprehensive strategy for growing your retirement savings and achieving long-term financial security.

Checklist of Key Items to Review When Considering Using the Wall Street Approach

When considering the Wall Street approach for your investments — which typically involves actively managing a portfolio to achieve higher returns through stock picking, market timing, and other strategic moves — it's essential to review various key aspects to make an informed decision.

Investment Goals: Clearly define your short-term and long-term investment goals and how they align with an active investment strategy.

Risk Tolerance: Evaluate your risk tolerance level. The Wall Street approach often involves higher risk compared to passive strategies.

Market Research: Be prepared to conduct extensive market research or rely on financial professionals to do so on your behalf.

Financial Knowledge: Assess your understanding of financial markets, investment strategies, and economic factors to ensure you can make informed decisions.

Active Management Costs: Understand the costs associated with active management, including higher fees for actively managed funds and potential transaction costs.

Performance Tracking: Know how to track and evaluate the performance of your investments against relevant benchmarks to determine the strategy's effectiveness.

Diversification: Ensure your portfolio is diversified to mitigate risk, even within an active management framework. Diversification can help protect against significant losses in any single investment.

Time Commitment: Acknowledge the time commitment required for active investment management, including regular portfolio reviews and adjustments.

Liquidity Needs: Consider your liquidity needs, as some active strategies may involve investments with extended holding periods or reduced access to cash.

Tax Implications: Be aware of the tax implications of active trading, including potential capital gains taxes on short-term profits.

Volatility Tolerance: Assess your comfort level with potential portfolio volatility, which is common in active management strategies.

Investment Advisor Selection: If employing a financial advisor or fund manager, carefully select a professional with a proven track record, transparent investment philosophy, and a straightforward approach to risk management.

Short-term vs. Long-term Focus: Decide whether you are focused on short-term gains or long-term growth, as this will influence your investment strategy and asset allocation.

Exit Strategy: Have a clear exit strategy for your investments, including criteria for selling underperforming assets or rebalancing your portfolio.

Emotional Discipline: Be prepared to maintain emotional discipline and avoid impulsive decisions based on market fluctuations or fear-driven reactions.

Regulatory and Legal Compliance: Ensure that your investment approach complies with all relevant regulations and legal standards, especially if working with investment advisors or brokers.

Continuous Learning: Stay informed about market trends, economic indicators, and financial news to make educated investment decisions.

Continuous learning can provide a competitive edge in active management.

Comparative Analysis: Regularly compare the performance of your active strategy with passive investment alternatives, such as index funds, to assess whether active management provides a better return on investment.

Rebalancing Strategy: Plan a strategy for rebalancing your portfolio to maintain alignment with your risk tolerance, goals, and asset allocation strategy.

Professional Advice: Consider consulting with a financial advisor for expert guidance, especially if you are new to active investment strategies or require help creating a personalized investment plan.

By thoroughly reviewing these items, you can make a more informed decision about whether the Wall Street approach aligns with your investment philosophy, financial goals, and risk tolerance. This approach requires commitment, emotional discipline, and continuous learning, but it can offer higher returns when executed effectively.

Index

12. Annuity to Supplement a 403b Plan
    - Complementing Retirement Savings
13. Converting a 403b Plan to an Annuity
    - Process and Implications
14. Consequences of Converting a 403b to Annuity
    - Impact on Retirement Income and Taxes
15. Annuity vs. Stock Market Considerations for Retirees
    - Security vs. Growth Potential
16. Percentage Allocation to Secure Annuity Investment vs. Stock for Retirees
    - Balancing Investment Choices
17. Investment in Annuity or Stock During a Down Market
    - Strategies for Market Downturns
18. Choosing a Financial Advisor or Annuity Broker
    - Selecting the Right Professional

Chapter 2: Life Insurance Options

1. Introduction to Life Insurance
    - Purpose and Importance
2. Types of Life Insurance
    - Term, Whole, Universal, Variable, Variable Universal
3. Explanation of Each Type of Life Insurance
    - Specific Features and Suitability
4. Usual and Customary Eligibility to Acquire Life Insurance
    - Age, Health, and Lifestyle Factors
5. Selling Life Insurance Policies
    - Life Settlements for Term and Permanent Policies
6. Life Settlements and Viatical Settlements
    - Definitions and Importance
7. Common Mistakes in Life Insurance
    - Underestimating Coverage Needs
8. Viatical Settlement Brokers
    - Role and Functions

9. Bundled Life Insurance for Death Benefit Planning
   - Strategy and Benefits
10. Examples and Formulas for Calculating   Benefits
   - Calculation of Bundled Plan Benefits
11. Using Cash Value Life Insurance to Build Wealth
   - Strategies for Financial Growth

Chapter 3: Alternative Investments

1. Introduction to Alternative Investments
   - Definition and Overview
2. What Is an Alternative Investment?
   - Description and Characteristics
3. Qualifications for Investors in an Alternative Investment
   - Accredited and Sophisticated Investor Status, Minimum Requirements
4. Types of Alternative Investments
   - Private Equity, Real Estate, Commodities, Hedge Funds, Private Debt, Venture Capital, Collectibles, Infrastructure
5. Advantages of Alternative Investments
   - Diversification, Potential for Higher Returns, Inflation Hedge, Risk Management
6. Risks and Challenges of Alternative Investments
   - Lack of Liquidity, Complexity, Higher Fees, Regulatory Compliance, Market Risk
7. Due Diligence in Alternative Investments
   - Steps for Assessment and Risk Management
8. Adding Alternatives to a Portfolio
   - Asset Allocation, Diversification, Monitoring, Rebalancing
9. Conclusion
   - Summary of Opportunities and Considerations

Chapter 4: Professional Advice

1. Building an Investment Portfolio Spreadsheet
   - Components and Tracking
2. Finding a Financial Advisor
   - Steps and Criteria
3. Fiduciary vs. Broker
   - Differences and Considerations
4. Working with a Fiduciary or Broker for Retirement Funds
   - Recommended Approach
5. Detecting Advisor's Interests
   - Identifying Commission Focus
6. Understanding Costs of Management
   - Comprehensive Overview
7. Testing a Financial Advisor
   - Evaluating Commitment and Expertise
8. Request for Proposal (RFP) for Financial Advisors
   - Creating and Utilizing an RFP
9. Dealing with Unfair Treatment by an Advisor
   - Steps for Resolution and Action
10. Conclusion
    - Importance of Selecting the Right Advisor

Chapter 5: Investment Options

1. Introduction to Investment Options
   - Overview and Importance
2. Dollar Cost Averaging (DCA)
   - Strategy and Advantages
3. Understanding Investment Corporate Bonds
   - Features and Considerations
4. Par Plus and Discount Prices of Corporate Bonds
   - Market Price Implications
5. Pros and Cons of CD Investments

- Advantages and Disadvantages
6. Understanding Municipal Bonds
   - Features and Investment Considerations
7. Conclusion
   - Summary of Investment Options

Chapter 6: Real Estate Investment

1. Introduction to Real Estate Investment
   - Overview and Benefits
2. Real Estate Investment vs. Stock Market over 20 Years
   - Comparative Analysis
3. Understanding Cap Rate
   - Definition and Calculation
4. Reserve Study for Homeowners Association or Condominium
   - Purpose and Components
5. Requesting a Copy of a Condominium Reserve Study
   - Process and Importance
6. Calculating a Reserve Study
   - Methodology and Example
7. Hard Money Loans
   - Characteristics and Use in Real Estate
8. Checking Individual Credit Risk
   - Assessment Methods
9. Conclusion
   - Summary of Real Estate Investment Strategies

Chapter 7: Social Security

1. Introduction to Social Security
   - Overview and Purpose
2. Social Security at Age 62 vs. Age 66
   - Benefits and Implications of Different Ages
3. Social Security Spouse Benefits

- Eligibility and Amounts
4. Conclusion
    - Summary of Social Security Considerations

Chapter 8: 401(k) and IRA

1. Introduction to 401(k) and IRA
    - Overview and Importance
2. Mandatory Withdrawal Age and Amounts
    - RMD Rules and Calculations
3. Transferring a 401(k) to an IRA
    - Steps and Considerations
4. IRA and 401(k) RMD Calculation Example
    - Example and Formula
5. Tax on Inherited Annuities and IRAs
    - Tax Implications and Rules
6. Conclusion
    - Summary of 401(k) and IRA Strategies

Chapter 9: Medicare

1. Introduction to Medicare
    - Overview and Purpose
2. Explanation of the Four Parts of Medicare
    - Coverage and Benefits
3. Medicare Options at Age 65
    - Enrollment Choices and Strategies
4. Medicare Supplemental vs. Advantage Plans
    - Comparison and Considerations
5. Medicare Costs by Location
    - Regional Variations
6. Conclusion
    - Summary of Medicare Planning

Chapter 10: Estate Planning

1. Introduction to Estate Planning
   - Importance and Objectives
2. Different Types of Trusts
   - Overview and Purposes
3. Value of Transfer Upon Death for Accounts
   - Benefits and Considerations
4. Choosing an Estate Planning Attorney
   - Criteria and Process
5. Conclusion
   - Summary of Estate Planning Strategies

Chapter 11: Invest in Yourself

1. Introduction to Investing in Yourself
   - Concept and Significance
2. The Importance of Self-Investment
   - Benefits and Areas of Focus
3. Ways to Invest in Yourself
   - Strategies and Activities
4. Balancing Self-Investment with Other Priorities
   - Integration and Time Management
5. Setting SMART Goals
   - Goal-Setting Framework
6. Building a Lifelong Learning Habit
   - Techniques and Importance
7. Conclusion
   - Summary of Personal Growth Strategies

Chapter 12: Saving for Children's Education

1. Introduction to Saving for Children's Education
   - Importance and Challenges
2. The Importance of Saving for Education
   - Benefits and Long-term Impact

Summary of Investment Strategies for Retirees

Dedication

Most people dream of a better future and pursue financial security. It is for those who understand that hard work is the foundation of success and that educated investing, coupled with the guidance of a trusted individual or group, serves as the compass guiding their journey.

I hope these pages serve as a steadfast companion to financial well-being. Determination fuels the hope that you can shape your financial destiny with sound advice and thoughtful decisions and provide a brighter future for yourselves and your loved ones.

May you find the answers you seek and the peace of mind from making informed choices. Dedication is the heartbeat of a financial journey, and proper guidance can lead to the economic freedom so richly deserved.

AJ Pelliccio